Step Up to **INTERMEDIATE**
Reading

MW01520418

Three Levels of Learning!

Carson-Dellosa Publishing Company, Inc. • Greensboro, North Carolina

Credits

Editor: Joey Bland

Layout Design: Lori Jackson

Inside Illustrations: Bill Neville, Lori Jackson

Cover Design: Lori Jackson

Cover Photo: © Brand X Pictures

This book has been correlated to state, national, and Canadian provincial standards. Visit *www.carsondellosa.com* to search for and view its correlations to your standards.

© 2008, Carson-Dellosa Publishing Company, Inc., Greensboro, North Carolina 27425. The purchase of this material entitles the buyer to reproduce worksheets and activities for classroom use only—not for commercial resale. Reproduction of these materials for an entire school or district is prohibited. No part of this book may be reproduced (except as noted above), stored in a retrieval system, or transmitted in any form or by any means (mechanically, electronically, recording, etc.) without the prior written consent of Carson-Dellosa Publishing Co., Inc.

Printed in the USA • All rights reserved.

ISBN: 978-1-60022-971-8

Table of Contents

Purpose

In any classroom, there are students who are working above and below grade level. These varying readiness levels present a daily challenge as teachers strive to meet the needs of every student. By differentiating instruction, teachers can provide modifications to meet these varying student needs. *Step Up to Reading: Intermediate* is a practical tool that teachers can use to help differentiate instruction and reinforce core skills.

What is Differentiated Instruction?

Differentiated instruction is a term used to describe an educational methodology that modifies instruction to accommodate the needs of individual students. These modifications involve offering multiple approaches to content, instruction, and assessment. Since students have varying ability levels, differentiation allows all students to maximize their strengths. Challenging and supporting all students through differentiated instruction results in increased motivation and student learning.

How Can Educators Effectively Differentiate Instruction?

Acknowledging that students learn in different ways is the first step toward differentiating instruction. Below are specific suggestions for differentiating instruction in the classroom:

1. Offer multiple methods for students to demonstrate success.

2. Provide a variety of materials at various levels that address various learning styles.

3. Tailor assignments to meet students' needs.

4. Provide appropriate learning experiences for all students.

5. Allow each student to work at his or her individual pace.

6. Support students by giving help as needed.

7. Provide learning tasks at an appropriate level of difficulty.

Step Up to Reading: Intermediate provides learning activities that offer students opportunities to develop needed skills and demonstrate individual strengths.

In This Book

Step Up to Reading: Intermediate is divided into core skills within each subject area. A detailed Table of Contents helps teachers identify and choose targeted skills.

Three leveled, reproducible activity sheets are provided for each core skill. Levels are indicated by the number of small circles at the bottom of each activity sheet:

- ⬤ Basic

- ⬤⬤ Intermediate

- ⬤⬤⬤ Challenging

How to Use This Book

- Tiered assignments are one way to provide tasks at varying levels. For each chosen skill, teachers should target a level based upon the readiness of an individual student. For example, assign basic tasks to struggling learners and assign challenging tasks to advanced learners. With this strategy, students focus on the same skill while working at their individual ability levels.

- Another approach is to have each student progress through the levels as he gains essential understandings or proficiency of each featured skill. This frequent, focused practice will help maximize student retention.

Other Suggestions

- As students progress through each level, document their progress on a generic class list. This provides additional documentation regarding student progress for administrators and parents.

- Use the readiness levels to form flexible groups for targeted instruction.

- Utilize the basic level skill sheets for student remediation.

- Review previously taught core skills with targeted learning activities.

- Form peer tutoring partnerships using students from basic/intermediate and intermediate/challenging level groups.

Name: _____ Date: _____

Prefixes

A **prefix** is a group of letters at the beginning of a word that changes the word's meaning. A prefix is added to a base word.

Example: pre + mature = premature

Add *un*, *re*, or *pre* to the word in parentheses to complete each sentence.

1. People once thought that the world was flat, but that was _____. (true)

2. He was _____ to lift the heavy weight. (able)

3. The library book was due, but Jim was able to _____ it. (new)

4. Jeff was _____ of what to do. (sure)

5. If you _____ people, you are forming an opinion about them before you know them. (judge)

6. Larry was sick and had to _____ behind. (main)

7. It is _____ to swim in that lake. (safe)

8. His father was _____ to hear his excuse. (willing)

9. Annie will _____ a poem called "Ode to a Robin." (cite)

10. My little brother is not old enough for kindergarten, so he is in _____. (school)

11. The refrigerator helps to _____ food. (serve)

12. The store will _____ your money if the toy does not work. (fund)

13. The storm wrecked our playhouse, so we had to _____ it. (build)

14. Vicki was _____ that she made only a C on her test. (happy)

15. Before baking the cake, we must _____ the oven. (heat)

Step Up to Reading · Intermediate · CD-104262 · © Carson-Dellosa

Prefixes

A **prefix** is a group of letters at the beginning of a word that changes the word's meaning. A prefix is added to a base word.

Example: pre + mature = premature

Complete the chart using the words from the list below. Write each word, its prefix, its base word, and its meaning. The prefixes and their meanings are in the word bank to the right. Use the word bank to help determine each word's meaning. The first one has been done for you.

pre	before
re	again
bi	two
un	not or undo
in	within
dis	not
non	not or reverse of
mis	wrong

bipolar   nonviolent

predetermine   misinterpret

untie   remove

prepay   disagree

return   intake

Word	Prefix	Base Word	Meaning
bipolar	bi	polar	occurring in two polar regions

Prefixes

A **prefix** is a group of letters at the beginning of a word that changes the word's meaning.

Example: im + probable = improbable

Read the prefixes and their meanings. Use them to complete the activities below.

mid—middle	post—after	super—beyond	uni—one; single
im—not	micro—very small	sub—below	de—do the opposite

Underline the base word in each word below. Then, write the meaning of the word.

1. midstream _____

2. decode _____

3. postgraduate _____

4. improper _____

5. unicolor _____

6. microscope _____

7. subzero _____

8. supernatural _____

Write a word from the word bank to complete each sentence.

microearthquakes	subcategory	midterm	unicycle
superhuman	immobilize	decipher	postmodern

9. There was a man at the circus who performed _____ feats.

10. You have to have good balance to ride a _____.

11. There are many _____ every day all over the world.

12. The enemy tried to _____ our messages during the war.

13. All courts are a _____ of the justice department.

14. The doctor put a splint on my finger to _____ it.

15. My sister studied hard for her _____ exam in chemistry.

16. There was a show of _____ art at the museum.

Suffixes

A **suffix** is a group of letters that is added to the end of a word to change the word's meaning.

Example: danger + ous = dangerous

Circle the word that correctly completes each sentence.

1. One day, Wendy and Wilma decided to go (camp, camping, camped).

2. They (pack, packing, packed) everything they needed in their truck.

3. Then, off they went to (hunt, hunting, hunted) for a good place to camp.

4. Finally, after looking for a long time, they (pick, picking, picked) a great campsite.

5. (Park, Parking, Parked) the truck was tricky because it was very slippery.

6. Wendy lost control and went (splash, splashing, splashed) into a pond.

7. Wilma ran over and quickly (pull, pulling, pulled) out Wendy.

8. Wendy's hat was (fill, filling, filled) with water and even a small fish.

9. After that, they both sat down on a rock to (rest, resting, rested).

10. Then, they (help, helping, helped) each other put up a tent and build a campfire.

11. After going (fish, fishing, fished), they cooked supper over the fire.

12. Wendy and Wilma hoped that their fun would never (end, ending, ended).

Suffixes

A **suffix** is a group of letters that is added to the end of a base word to change the word's meaning. Suffixes may also change a word's part of speech. For example, a verb may become a noun, a noun may become an adjective, or an adjective may become an adverb.

Examples: walk + er = walker; verb to noun (I walk every day. I am a walker)

star + less = starless; noun to adjective (I cannot see a single star. It is a cloudy, starless night.)

happy + ly = happily; adjective to adverb (John is a happy boy. He skipped happily on his way.)

Complete the chart using the suffixes from the list below. Use each suffix only once.

ment—concrete result

ist—person who does

less—without

able—capable

al—related to, like

ful—full of

ward—in the direction of

ship—state; condition

Base Word	Part of Speech	Base Word + Suffix	Part of Speech
1. entertain	verb	entertainment	noun
2. hand			
3. out			
4. thought			
5. active			
6. excite			
7. relation			
8. music			

Suffixes

A **suffix** is a group of letters that is added to the end of a base word to change the word's meaning.

Example: danger + ous = dangerous

Read the suffixes and their meanings. Use them to complete the activities below.

ly—manner; relating   ous—have qualities of

ish—likeness   al—related to; time

ist—one who does or is; skilled at   ship—quality of or having the office of

Underline the base word in each word. Then, write the meaning of the word. Use a dictionary to help you.

1. fiendish   _____

2. leadership   _____

3. courageous   _____

4. sweetly   _____

5. frontal   _____

6. lobbyist   _____

Use the words from the word bank to complete the paragraph.

timely	reddish	abruptly	mechanical	carefully
specialist	happily	resident	generous	patiently

The _____ of the _____

apartment building was a _____ in his field at the hospital.

On the way to work, his car stopped _____ because of

_____ problems. He _____

waited for a tow truck. The serviceman _____ loaded

the car onto his truck. The specialist _____ found a ride to

work from a _____ friend. The specialist's car was fixed in

a _____ manner.

Name: _____ Date: _____

Base Words, Prefixes, and Suffixes

Base words are the root words that can be used to make other words. For example, helpful—the root word is help.

Prefixes are letters added in front of a base word to change the meaning of the base word. For example, rewrite—the prefix **re** changes the meaning of the base word write.

Suffixes are letters added to the end of a base word to change the meaning of the base word. For example: healthy—the suffix **y** changes the meaning of the base word health.

Decide what part of each word is bold. Write *base word*, *prefix*, or *suffix*.

1. **punish**ment _____

2. **dis**appear _____

3. pre**soak** _____

4. place**ment** _____

5. color**less** _____

6. **sick**ness _____

7. fool**ish** _____

8. **re**fill _____

9. **un**sure _____

10. dark**ness** _____

11. **pre**cook _____

12. proud**ly** _____

13. **dis**trust _____

14. **friend**ly _____

15. **sugar**less _____

16. brown**ish** _____

17. pre**pay** _____

18. lone**ly** _____

Step Up to Reading · Intermediate · CD-104262 · © Carson-Dellosa

Base Words, Prefixes, and Suffixes

Base words are the root words that can be used to make other words. For example, <u>helpful</u>—the root word is <u>help</u>.

Prefixes are letters added in front of a base word to change the meaning of the base word. For example, <u>rewrite</u>—the prefix **re** changes the meaning of the base word <u>write</u>.

Suffixes are letters added to the end of a base word to change the meaning of the base word. For example: health<u>y</u>—the suffix **y** changes the meaning of the base word <u>health</u>.

Read the prefixes and suffixes and their meanings. Use them to write the meanings of the words below.

Prefixes	Suffixes
re—back or again	ment—the act, result, or product of
dis—away, apart, the opposite of	ish—of or belonging to; like or about
un—opposite, not, or lack of	less—without, or not
pre—before	

1. punishment _____

2. disappear _____

3. presoak _____

4. rewind _____

5. colorless _____

6. precooked _____

7. unsure _____

8. brownish _____

Base Words, Prefixes, and Suffixes

Base words are the root words that can be used to make other words. For example, <u>helpful</u>—the root word is <u>help</u>.

Prefixes are letters added in front of a base word to change the meaning of the base word. For example, <u>rewrite</u>—the prefix **re** changes the meaning of the base word <u>write</u>.

Suffixes are letters added to the end of a base word to change the meaning of the base word. For example: heal<u>thy</u>—the suffix **y** changes the meaning of the base word <u>health</u>.

Complete the chart by separating each word into its prefix, base word, and suffix. The first one has been done for you.

Remember: Sometimes, the silent *e* is removed from the base word when a suffix is added. For example, remove becomes removable.

Word	Prefix	Base Word	Suffix
1. refreshment	re	fresh	ment
2. undependable			
3. enlargement			
4. renewable			
5. disapproving			
6. untruthful			
7. prearrangement			
8. untouchable			
9. enforcer			
10. returnable			
11. delightful			
12. preoccupied			
13. enlisting			
14. indispensable			
15. disgraceful			
16. unlawful			
17. biodegradable			
18. recyclable			

Words with Multiple Meanings

Some words have more than one meaning. The **context** of a sentence will help you determine the correct meaning of the word.

Example: The cowboy wore spurs and <u>chaps</u> when he went on a roundup.

Possible definitions: 1. leather leggings connected by a belt worn over regular pants; 2. men (The sentence gives you clues to determine that the first definition is being used.)

Write two sentences for each word that use different meanings for the words.

1. park

    1. _____

        _____

    2. _____

        _____

2. hand

    1. _____

        _____

    2. _____

        _____

3. bat

    1. _____

        _____

    2. _____

        _____

4. set

    1. _____

        _____

    2. _____

        _____

Words with Multiple Meanings

Some words have more than one meaning. The **context** of a sentence will help you determine the correct meaning of the word.

Example: The cowboy wore spurs and <u>chaps</u> when he went on a roundup.

Possible definitions: 1. leather leggings connected by a belt worn over regular pants; 2. men (The sentence gives you clues to determine that the first definition is being used.)

Match the definitions from the bottom of the page with the words. Each word will have more than one definition.

Example: punch ___*X, Y, Z*___

Mini-Dictionary: X. to strike

Y. a tool for making a hole

Z. a drink made of several ingredients

1.	palm	_____	2.	harp	_____
3.	fiddle	_____	4.	prompt	_____
5.	court	_____	6.	sore	_____
7.	vessel	_____	8.	glare	_____
9.	mask	_____	10.	cabinet	_____

A. meeting room in a king's residence
B. a stringed instrument played with a bow
C. to dwell on a subject for a lengthy amount of time
D. a tube in the body in which body fluid travels
E. flat part of the hand between the bases of the fingers and the wrist
F. a face used for disguise
G. a shine with a harsh, brilliant light
H. move hands and fingers restlessly
I. tender, painful
J. cupboard with doors and shelves
K. ready; on time

L. enclosed area where some ball games are played
M. to assist an actor by saying his next words
N. type of tree
O. a plucked string instrument
P. a large boat
Q. stare angrily
R. a place where judges hear cases
S. a body of advisers to a head of state
T. a container for holding something
U. angry
V. to cover up; hide something
W. a spot on the body

Words with Multiple Meanings

Some words have more than one meaning. The **context** of a sentence will help you determine the correct meaning of the word.

Example: The cowboy wore spurs and <u>chaps</u> when he went on a roundup.

Possible definitions: 1. leather leggings connected by a belt worn over regular pants; 2. men (The sentence gives you clues to determine that the first definition is being used.)

Circle the definition of the bold word in each sentence.

1. The featherbed was warm but very **light** to carry.

   A. set fire to   B. lamp   C. not heavy

2. Father took Jenny's picture riding **bareback** on her new pony.

   A. on a horse without a saddle   B. nothing covering the back   C. went back

3. Jerry ordered **lean** meat from the butcher.

   A. rest against   B. containing little fat   C. containing little nourishment

4. A woodwind player keeps extra **reeds** handy in case the one she is using splits.

   A. tall grasses   B. arrows   C. thin pieces of cane or metal attached to an air opening

5. The new **bureau** was put in Tim's room on the second floor.

   A. department of government   B. chest of drawers   C. administrative unit

6. The teacher asked Susan to **divide** 105 by 15.

   A. separate into equal parts   B. opposite of multiply   C. distribute parts

7. The voice teacher had her student sing the **scale** as a warm-up exercise.

   A. machine to measure weight   B. graduated series   C. climb

8. David did the **right** thing when he turned in the wallet he found.

   A. proper   B. opposite of left   C. show ownership

9. Christy always **trails** behind looking for wildlife when we go hiking.

   A. paths   B. pursues   C. lags

10. The boys were **loafers** who put off raking leaves and doing other chores to go fishing and sit around at the lake.

    A. shoes   B. lazy people   C. loaves of bread

Synonyms

A **synonym** is a word that may be used in place of another word without changing the meaning of a sentence.

Examples: The old man carried all of his money in a brown <u>sack</u>.
The old man carried all of his money in a brown <u>bag</u>.
The old man carried all of his money in a brown <u>pouch</u>.

Complete the puzzle by matching each bold word below with its synonym from the word bank.

remember
well-known
starving
smart
great
crowd
doctor
grabbed
bite

Across

2. My dog is so **intelligent** that he learned three new tricks in one day.
3. Your birthday party was **superb**!
5. Do you **recall** the phone number?
7. My mom took me to our **physician** when I got sick.

Down

1. On Monday, a **famous** artist will visit our school.
2. I was **famished**, so I ate two plates of spaghetti.
3. My aunt **grasped** the railing as she came down the stairs.
4. There was a huge **mob** of fans outside the concert.
6. Jack's puppy likes to **gnaw** on the bone.

Synonyms

A **synonym** is a word that may be used in place of another word without changing the meaning of a sentence.

Examples: My dog is so <u>smart</u> that he learned three new tricks in one day.
My dog is so <u>intelligent</u> that he learned three new tricks in one day.
My dog is so <u>brilliant</u> that he learned three new tricks in one day.

Complete each sentence by choosing a synonym from the word bank for each word in parentheses.

required	country	finished	erected	place
pupils	plans	sprinkling	trip	welcomed

1. The fourth grade was going on a two-day _____ to learn more about their state's history. (journey)

2. Everyone was excited about the trip and knew that good _____ must be made in order to have a successful adventure. (arrangements)

3. When planning, they considered the weather, _____ clothing, and how much money they would need. (necessary)

4. The day the trip began, it was _____ in the morning. (drizzling)

5. But, that did not bother the _____ as they boarded the bus in their raincoats. (students)

6. The bus traveled through one _____ town after another until it reached the State History Museum. (rural)

7. Once inside, they were _____ by Mrs. Handler, a guide, who took them through the museum. (greeted)

8. The students learned that the state's capitol had been _____ almost 200 years earlier. (built)

9. After the guide _____ the lesson, the students thanked her and left to continue their trip. (completed)

10. As the bus drove to the next _____, the students ate the lunches they had prepared before leaving home that morning. (stop)

Synonyms

A **synonym** is a word that may be used in place of another word without changing the meaning of a sentence.

Examples: Do you <u>remember</u> the phone number?
Do you <u>recall</u> the phone number?
Do you <u>recollect</u> the phone number?

Write the word that is not a synonym for the first word.

1. **old**   elderly   young   antique   aged   _____

2. **intelligent**   smart   forgetful   clever   brainy   _____

3. **chuckle**   laugh   snicker   moan   giggle   _____

4. **purpose**   perhaps   aim   goal   mission   _____

5. **screen**   hide   conceal   cover   view   _____

6. **mend**   repair   fix   rip   patch   _____

7. **cry**   weep   laugh   sob   wail   _____

Circle the synonym in parentheses for each bold word in the sentences.

8. We were **floating** down the river on our inner tubes. (gliding, sailing)

9. I was so **excited** about going to the beach that I could not sleep. (anxious, nervous)

10. My brother **collects** autographs of movie stars. (gathers, finds)

11. Whitney has been **late** to class several times this year. (tardy, slow)

12. Our class needs to inflate 50 balloons for the **celebration**. (party, event)

13. Juan needed a **plain** sheet of paper to draw his picture. (simple, ordinary)

14. Could I have a **piece** of your delicious apple pie? (section, slice)

Antonyms

An **antonym** is a word that has the opposite meaning of another word.

Examples: John <u>started</u> his homework.
John <u>finished</u> his homework.

Find the antonym in the word bank for each bold word. Write its letter on the basket of the matching balloon.

A.	lower	C.	dull	E.	fresh
B.	simple	D.	scatter	F.	tidy

1. I watched the squirrel **collect** nuts before the snowstorm hit.

2. This bread must be old. It tastes **stale**.

3. I wish that I had practiced more. The test was **difficult** for me.

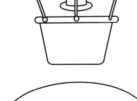

4. Painting is fun, but it can be **messy** at times.

5. Before the game, they always **raise** the flag.

6. The stars are **bright** in the sky tonight.

Antonyms

An **antonym** is a word that has the opposite meaning of another word.

Examples: Billy was <u>elated</u> about his grade on the science exam.
Billy was <u>depressed</u> about his grade on the science exam.

Read the pairs of sentences. Circle the word in the first sentence that is the antonym for the bold word in the second sentence.

1. The air was moist and cool after the heavy rain last night.
   Once the sun was out for a couple of hours, the air seemed to be **dry**.

2. A stray dog was enclosed in a pen until the owner came to get her.
   When the dog was **released** to her owner, she jumped up to lick him.

3. Dad was ignorant about the driving laws when he visited England.
   He became **knowledgeable** quickly by reading a book of the rules.

4. Dripping water from our roof will freeze in the winter to make icicles.
   Sometimes, it is spring before the icicles **thaw** and disappear.

5. Madame Proctor purchased a valuable diamond at the auction.
   The diamond turned out to be **worthless** when she discovered that it was a fake.

6. Ben enjoys Saturdays because he goes to his grandparents' farm.
   He **dislikes** it when it is time to leave them and their farm animals.

7. Hurricanes and tornadoes can destroy anything in their paths.
   It sometimes takes months to **repair** the damage they cause.

8. When Nancy is at the park, she often plays on the swings.
   She **seldom** has to wait to take her turn.

9. It was foolish of Ricky not to study for the science test.
   He wished that he had been more **sensible** and had studied for it when he saw his grade.

10. When Cathy woke, she had to face reality.
    She realized that her dreams the night before were just **fantasy**.

Antonyms

An **antonym** is a word that has the opposite meaning of another word.

Examples: Mother <u>bought</u> an antique quilt at the flea market.
Mother <u>sold</u> an antique quilt at the flea market.

Read each pair of sentences and decide whether the bold words are antonyms.
Circle *yes* or *no*.

1. When the ship was in port, the deckhands **unloaded** the freight.
   Deckhands **loaded** the cargo before the passengers boarded the ship.

   yes   no

2. Natalie was **satisfied** with the way the baker decorated the cake.
   The baker was **displeased** with the decorated cake.

   yes   no

3. Work was being done constantly on the old house to **maintain** its value.
   There was an order to **preserve** the old courthouse when all of the other old buildings around it were demolished.

   yes   no

4. Everyone **present** at the city council meeting voiced opinions about the new highway going through town.
   Bert was **absent** the day the council members went to the wildlife refuge.

   yes   no

5. The boy **staggered** when he got off of the merry-go-round.
   Martha **tottered** down the steps after riding the roller coaster.

   yes   no

Homophones

Homophones are words that are pronounced the same but are spelled differently and have different meanings.

Examples: Mother went <u>to</u> the meeting at school.
Father went <u>too</u>.
The <u>two</u> of them met my teacher.

Complete each sentence using one of the homophones in parentheses. Then, write a sentence using the other homophone.

1. The _____ of the tree hung low over the sidewalk. (bough, bow)

   _____

2. Jane had been sick for more than a week and was _____ staying in bed. (board, bored)

   _____

3. The wranglers watched the _____ on the range. (heard, herd)

   _____

4. Donna and Tom walked _____ the passage that led into the cave. (threw, through)

   _____

5. An _____ is a type of boat. (ark, arc)

   _____

6. In _____ shop did you find your new shoes? (witch, which)

   _____

7. Father stopped and asked the _____ to the stadium. (way, weigh)

   _____

8. The campers put a _____ over the fire and put a pot of water on it to boil. (great, grate)

   _____

Homophones

Homophones are words that are pronounced the same but are spelled differently and have different meanings.

Examples: My aunt and uncle said that <u>they're</u> coming to visit.
Please take this box over <u>there</u>.
Mom does not want it to be in <u>their</u> way.

Complete each sentence using a set of homophones from the word bank.

capitol	threw	heal	principle
capital	through	heel	principal
chute	cord	I'll	patience
shoot	chord	isle	patients
		aisle	

1. _____ walk down the tree-covered _____

    on the tropical _____.

2. I want to _____ your picture when you race

    down the water _____.

3. When the pianist hit the song's first _____, an

    electrical _____ shorted and the concert hall went dark.

4. The doctor's _____ had little _____

    when they learned that the doctor would be an hour late.

5. We drove to our state's _____, Springfield, Illinois,

    and we went on a tour of the _____.

6. Tina _____ a ball _____

    a tunnel for her dog to chase.

7. The one _____ that the _____

    expected the students to maintain was "always do your best."

8. John had a sore on his _____ that would not _____.

Homophones

Homophones are words that are pronounced the same but are spelled differently and have different meanings.

Examples: There is a <u>frieze</u> that goes across the front of city hall.
Water will <u>freeze</u> when the air temperature goes below 32°F or 0°C.
The game warden at the wildlife refuge <u>frees</u> injured animals when they are well enough to live in the wild on their own.

Complete each sentence using the correct homophone in parentheses.

1. The Native Americans taught the Pilgrims how to plant _____. (maze, maize)

2. The _____ of your company is requested at Sampson's party. (presence, presents)

3. The nurse had trouble finding my _____ when he drew my blood. (vein, vane)

4. We took a _____ ship through the Panama Canal. (crews, cruise)

5. Erica won a gold _____ in ice-skating for the third year in a row. (medal, metal, meddle)

6. The old _____ tree was struck by lightning. (beach, beech)

7. That post is _____, so all of the furniture must be placed around it. (stationery, stationary)

8. A traditional _____ was held for the bishop when he passed away. (right, rite, write)

9. When we make bread, we let it rise and then we _____ it. (need, knead)

10. They cleared the grocery _____ in order to make room for the canned soup display. (isle, I'll, aisle)

11. I had never seen anyone play the _____ until I went to the concert. (lyre, liar)

12. Father received a letter that used _____ wax to secure the envelope closed. (ceiling, sealing)

Analogies

Analogies are one way to compare and analyze words. The best way to solve an analogy is to look at only the first two words. How are they related to each other? Then, apply that same relationship to the next set of words.

Example: <u>Fish</u> is to <u>water</u> as <u>camel</u> is to _____. (Fish is related to water because it is its habitat. What is a camel's habitat? The answer is <u>desert</u>.)

Complete each analogy using a word from the tic-tac-toe board below. Then, mark X or O over the word on the board to find whether X or O wins.

1. Circle is to sphere as square is to _____.
   Mark X.

2. Yellow is to banana as orange is to _____.
   Mark O.

3. Food is to pantry as clothes is to _____.
   Mark X.

4. Two is to pair as twelve is to _____.
   Mark O.

5. Limb is to tree as leg is to _____.
   Mark X.

6. Corner is to square as point is to _____.
   Mark O.

7. Bucket is to pail as path is to _____.
   Mark X.

8. Shovel is to dig as broom is to _____.
   Mark O.

star	sweep	pumpkin
closet	dozen	cube
chair	floor	trail

Analogies

Analogies are one way to compare and analyze words. What are the relationships in the examples?

Examples: <u>Trunk</u> is to <u>tree</u> as <u>stem</u> is to <u>flower</u>.
 <u>Run</u> is to <u>ran</u> as <u>sleep</u> is to <u>slept</u>.
 <u>Puppy</u> is to <u>dog</u> as <u>kid</u> is to <u>goat</u>.

Write the word from the word bank that completes each analogy.

trout	car	tornado	cows	fingers
canyon	addition	keys	safe	store
blue	squirrel	stand	train	tropics

1. Subtraction is to _____ as division is to multiplication.

2. Anchor is to ship as brake is to _____ .

3. Humidity is to arid as _____ are to desert.

4. _____ is to tracks as bus is to road.

5. _____ is to river as dolphin is to ocean.

6. Deep is to high as _____ is to mountain.

7. _____ are to hands as toes are to feet.

8. Key is to door as combination is to _____ .

9. Sapphire is to _____ as emerald is to green.

10. Aisle is to _____ as path is to woods.

11. Violin is to bow as piano is to _____ .

12. Cheese is to mouse as acorn is to _____ .

13. Barn is to coop as _____ are to chickens.

14. Freeze is to froze as _____ is to stood.

15. Rain is to monsoon as wind is to _____ .

Analogies

Analogies are one way to compare and analyze words. Analogies show relationships.

Example: <u>Anchor</u> is to <u>ship</u> as <u>brake</u> is to <u>car</u>.

Analogies may be written this way: Blue is to green as sky is to grass.
They may also be written this way: blue : green : : sky : grass

Complete each analogy with a word from the word bank.

1. rind : _____ : : skin : apple

2. day : week : : month : _____

3. _____ : niece : : uncle : nephew

4. push : shove : : pull : _____

5. read : _____ : : book : paper

6. palm : hand : : _____ : foot

7. _____ : down : : ascend : descend

8. collar : _____ : : cuff : wrist

9. when : time : : where : _____

10. celery : _____ : : lettuce : leaf

11. two : _____ : : four : eight

12. flower : pot : : _____ : trellis

13. clear : muddy : : _____ : cloudy

14. _____ : thirsty : : food : beverage

15. water : _____ : : ice : rink

16. carpenter : wood : : _____ : stone

17. golf : course : : tennis : _____

18. painting : art : : skeleton : _____

19. bear : cub : : _____ : kid

20. _____ : lions : : gaggle : geese

goat
stalk
vine
hungry
lemon
transparent
anatomy
mason
write
neck
sole
up
year
four
aunt
pool
haul
court
pride
place

Similes and Metaphors

Similes and **metaphors** compare two things. Similes use words such as *like* or *as* to compare the two unrelated things. Metaphors do not.

Example of a simile: She was <u>as</u> clever <u>as</u> a fox.

Example of a metaphor: His teeth were shiny pearls.

Determine whether each sentence is a simile or a metaphor. If the sentence is a simile, write *S*. If it is a metaphor, write *M*.

_____ 1. The fruit salad is a rainbow of colors.

_____ 2. The pineapple slices are as yellow as the sun.

_____ 3. The strawberries are little red ladybugs.

_____ 4. The grapes are light green globes.

_____ 5. The marshmallows look like tiny white clouds.

_____ 6. The delicious salad tasted like summer.

Complete each phrase to create your own simile or metaphor.

7. The shiny nickel is like _____.

8. The soft lamb's fur was _____.

9. The butterfly was as colorful as _____.

10. The trickling stream was _____.

11. The cute bunny is _____.

12. Jeremy was as fast as _____.

Similes and Metaphors

Similes and **metaphors** compare two things. Similes use words such as *like* or *as* to compare the two unrelated things. Metaphors do not.

Example of a simile: Ronnie runs <u>like</u> a deer.

Example of a metaphor: The moon was a lamp lighting up the night.

Complete each simile using a word from the word bank.

rocket	mouse	swings	shiny	midnight	flat

1. The theater was as black as _____ before the movie started.

2. Jayla was as quiet as a _____ as she studied for the test.

3. My dad's new shoes are as _____ as a new penny.

4. The airless ball is now as _____ as a pancake.

5. Taylor's brother _____ like a monkey on the jungle gym.

6. The first batter's baseball flew like a _____ out of the ballpark.

Circle the two words that are being compared in each metaphor. Then, write what about the two words is being compared.

7. The row of trees are soldiers standing at attention.

    _____

8. Looking down from the airplane, the cars were ants crawling along the highway.

    _____

9. Twenty circus clowns were sardines packed in one car.

    _____

10. The shadows were ghosts dancing on the sunlit lawn.

    _____

11. The sound of waves lapping the shore reminded me of dogs getting a long drink.

    _____

12. The fans' stamping feet in the bleachers were drums beating inside my head.

    _____

Similes and Metaphors

Similes and **metaphors** are comparisons. Similes use *like*, *as*, or *than* to compare two things. Metaphors are implied comparisons. Both compare two unlike things.

Example of a simile: The runner ran <u>like</u> a deer on the last lap of the race.

Example of a metaphor: His hair was an uncombed, stringy mop.

Determine whether each comparison is a simile or metaphor. Write *simile* or *metaphor*.

1. Meg babbled on and on like a brook about her baby brother. _____

2. The boys' eyes were as big as saucers when the magician pulled a mouse out of Larry's shirt. _____

3. Some news travels like the wind. _____

4. This piece of candy is as hard as a rock. _____

5. The moon was a bald man's head. _____

6. The dark clouds were dragons spitting fire. _____

7. Joe is a dirty rat to squeal about the surprise. _____

8. The fog is as thick as pea soup. _____

9. The soldier stood straight as an arrow. _____

10. The puppy ran around like a tornado. _____

11. After the fireworks, the sky was a red ceiling. _____

12. After the blizzard, the highway was as smooth as glass. _____

13. The package was as light as a feather. _____

14. The flower bed is a rainbow on the ground. _____

15. The lawyer was a tiger concerning his client's innocence. _____

16. The soprano in the opera sings like a canary. _____

Idioms

An **idiom** is a phrase that states one thing but means another.

Example: It was <u>raining cats and dogs</u>. (The sentence means that it was raining hard.)

Draw a line to match each idiom with its meaning.

1. I can do math problems standing on my head.

2. Who let the cat out of the bag?

3. Charlie is a chip off the old block.

4. Jenna will sleep like a log.

5. She is the top banana in her class.

6. Cindy is the apple of her mother's eye.

7. Now, he is in the doghouse!

8. I would like to add my two cents.

9. Do not cry over spilled milk.

10. You can catch more flies with honey than with vinegar.

Do not get upset over what cannot be changed.

She is her mother's favorite person.

You will have more friends if you are nice.

I know math very well.

I would like to give my opinion.

Who told the secret?

He is in big trouble!

She will sleep very well tonight.

She is the smartest child in her class.

He is just like his father.

Idioms

An **idiom** is a figure of speech. It is often a phrase. It says one thing but means another.

Example: It was <u>raining cats and dogs</u>. (The sentence means that it was raining hard.)

Write the letter for the meaning of the bold idiom in each sentence.

_____ 1. He is a **big cheese** at the high school.

    A. cafeteria worker   B. principal   C. very important person

_____ 2. When I met the doctor, she gave me a **dead fish** handshake.

    A. limp   B. strong   C. wet

_____ 3. Tommy would **give you the shirt off his back**, if necessary.

    A. lend you a shirt   B. help anyway he could   C. keep you warm

_____ 4. She did not talk about her family because she did not want to reveal **the skeletons in her closet**.

    A. her family secrets   B. where she kept trash   C. the end of a scary story

_____ 5. My dad is the **top dog** at the factory.

    A. loudest one   B. parts supplier   C. one in charge; boss

_____ 6. Let us **bury the hatchet** and get on with our lives.

    A. forget the past   B. stop chopping trees   C. go to the movies

_____ 7. The kid who always hides my books is a real **thorn in my side**.

    A. prickly plant   B. bothersome person   C. ticklish

_____ 8. I really **put my foot in my mouth** when I offered to bake all of the cakes for the bake sale.

    A. spoke before thinking   B. hurt my mouth   C. was angry

_____ 9. The girl with the whiny voice **is not my cup of tea**.

    A. makes the wrong tea   B. is not my kind of person   C. scares me

_____ 10. The **sky is the limit** when it comes to how many Girl Scout cookies you sell.

    A. boxes are blue   B. cookies are delicious   C. number is limitless

Name: _____ Date: _____

Idioms

An **idiom** is a figure of speech. It is often a phrase. It says one thing but means another.

Example: There was a long silence before Sam <u>broke the ice</u> by telling a funny story. (Broke the ice means made everyone relax.)

Write the letter for the meaning of the bold idiom in each sentence.

A. a different subject
C. out of place
E. had the same problem
G. lost the opportunity
I. was undecided

B. tell a secret
D. talk a lot
F. did it right
H. cause trouble
J. try out something

_____ 1. The doctor was **a fish out of water** when he was at a meeting for hospital accountants.

_____ 2. The cousins at the family reunion stayed up late to **shoot the breeze**.

_____ 3. The factory worker did not want to **make waves** for fear that he might lose his job.

_____ 4. The school's finance committee was discussing what playground equipment to buy when Mrs. Jones raised a question about buying books for the library. The chairperson of the committee said, "That is **a horse of a different color.**"

_____ 5. You should **test the waters** before making a major decision.

_____ 6. The food committee **hit the nail on the head** when it planned the menu for the school picnic.

_____ 7. Everyone on the highway **was in the same boat** when the truck carrying eggs overturned during rush hour.

_____ 8. My father was angry at himself because he **missed the boat** when he did not buy property on the lake at half of the current cost.

_____ 9. Aunt Barbara **ran hot and cold** about the candidates running for office.

_____ 10. Do not **let the cat out of the bag** about the surprise party!

Alphabetizing

Most reference work requires the skill of **alphabetizing**. Dictionaries, encyclopedias, and other reference materials are organized alphabetically.

Sometimes, it is necessary to look at only the first letter of each word when alphabetizing a list.

Example: anteater donkey lizard whale

Other times, the first letter of each word is the same and you have to look at the second letter.

Example: calendar ceiling chime cliff creek

When the first two letters of each word are the same, you have to look at the third letter.

Example: alignment alligator allotment aluminum

And, when the first three letters of each word are the same, you have to look at the fourth letter.

Example: exception excitement exclamation excretion

Put each list of words in alphabetical order by numbering the words 1–5.

1.		2.		3.	
_____	brag	_____	brittle	_____	weary
_____	speak	_____	freeze	_____	trick
_____	dreary	_____	beast	_____	salmon
_____	united	_____	yellow	_____	tragic
_____	spool	_____	frown	_____	quarrel
4.		**5.**		**6.**	
_____	cabin	_____	grease	_____	dive
_____	spend	_____	gripe	_____	dungeon
_____	shallow	_____	turkey	_____	dump
_____	universe	_____	evening	_____	double
_____	casement	_____	grand	_____	dream

Name: _____ Date: _____

Alphabetizing

Most reference work requires the skill of **alphabetizing**. Dictionaries, encyclopedias, and other reference materials are organized alphabetically.

Sometimes, it is necessary to look at only the first letter of each word when alphabetizing a list.

Example: alligator crocodile iguana turtle

Other times, the first letter of each word is the same and you have to look at the second letter.

Example: raspberries reasonable rifle roast runt

When the first two letters of each word are the same, you have to look at the third letter.

Example: thanks these three thump

And, when the first three letters of each word are the same, you have to look at the fourth letter.

Example: except excite exclaim excrete

Put each list of words in alphabetical order by numbering the words 1–5.

1. _____ cannibal		2. _____ shrink		3. _____ elevate	
_____ creek		_____ shirt		_____ eventually	
_____ ceiling		_____ sheet		_____ elementary	
_____ chime		_____ shut		_____ evaporate	
_____ chill		_____ shout		_____ evaluate	
4. _____ cranium		5. _____ planet		6. _____ aluminum	
_____ crawl		_____ placement		_____ alignment	
_____ crater		_____ plural		_____ allotment	
_____ crash		_____ pleasant		_____ alligator	
_____ crew		_____ plant		_____ alphabet	

Alphabetizing

Most reference work requires the skill of **alphabetizing**. Dictionaries, encyclopedias, and other reference materials are organized alphabetically.

Sometimes, it is necessary to look at only the first letter of each word when alphabetizing a list.

Example: banana grapefruit lime peach

Other times, the first letter of each word is the same and you have to look at the second letter.

Example: shift sign slant spot

When the first two letters of each word are the same, you have to look at the third letter.

Example: coat color company corn

And, when the first three letters of each word are the same, you have to look at the fourth letter.

Example: process program promise proud

Put each list of words in alphabetical order by numbering the words 1–5.

1. ____ antilog   2. ____ most   3. ____ anchor   4. ____ contest
    ____ antigen   ____ mosaic   ____ annex   ____ contact
    ____ antic   ____ mosquito   ____ analyze   ____ contrary
    ____ antique   ____ mosey   ____ anytime   ____ confusion
    ____ antidote   ____ moss   ____ angel   ____ continue

5. ____ require   6. ____ horn   7. ____ push   8. ____ decide
    ____ resist   ____ hoist   ____ pulley   ____ diesel
    ____ reply   ____ honey   ____ public   ____ differ
    ____ reserve   ____ hound   ____ pudding   ____ digest
    ____ represent   ____ hoop   ____ purple   ____ dictate

Dictionary Skills

A **dictionary** is a book that does not tell a story, but instead lists words and their meanings. A word you look up in a dictionary is called an **entry word**, and its meaning is called the **definition**. If the word has more than one meaning, its definitions will be numbered.

Use the dictionary entries below to answer the questions.

1. Which definition best fits the word *cry* as it is used in the following sentence? The little girl *cried* out for her mother. Definition number _____

2. List other forms of the word *cute*. _____

3. Which part of speech is the word *cream*? _____

4. Which definition best fits the word *crook* as it is used in the following sentence? The *crook* stole the diamond. Definition number _____

5. What is the definition of the word *dark*? _____

_____

cream \'krEm\ *noun*, plural **creams** the yellowish-white part of milk (Butter is made from *cream*.)

crook \'kruk\ *noun*, plural **crooks** **1.** a bent part; curve (My umbrella was in the *crook* of my arm.) **2.** a shepherd's staff with a hook at the top **3.** a person who is not honest

cry \'krI\ *verb* **cried**; **crying** **1.** to shed tears; weep (Don't make the baby *cry*.) **2.** to call out loudly; shout (I heard the people in the burning building *cry* for help.)

cute \'kyüt\ *adjective* **cuter**, **cutest** delightful or pretty (That is a very *cute* puppy.)

dark \dark\ *adjective* having little or no light (The night was *dark* since the clouds covered the moon.)

¹dash \dash\ *verb* **dashed**, **dashing** **1.** to move fast; rush (If I am late, I *dash* to my classroom.) **2.** to destroy or ruin (If I hurt my ankle, I will *dash* my hopes of running in the race.)

²dash *noun* **1.** a fast movement or sudden rush (I made a *dash* for the waiting bus.) **2.** a small amount

Dictionary Skills

A **dictionary** is a book that does not tell a story, but instead lists words and their meanings. A word you look up in a dictionary is called an **entry word**, and its meaning is called the **definition**. If the word has more than one meaning, its definitions will be numbered.

Guide words are the two words at the top of each dictionary page. Any entry word listed on that page will fall alphabetically between the guide words.

Examples: choice—chop   grand—grape   peddle—peg
            choose   granola   peep

Circle the entry words that would be found on the page with each set of guide words.

1. badger—bird	2. ink—javelin	3. penguin—play
bald	impossible	platypus
black	item	peach
baby	jamboree	please
beach	jawless	peace
bicycle	irate	photograph
braid	inch	pepper

4. riot—rustic	5. masquerade—mill	6. send—sharp
risky	mask	simple
romp	matter	shaft
rumor	money	settle
reaper	mice	shave
rouse	mosque	select
reason	mile	sleek

7. thermos—time	8. angora—archery	9. comma—cone
thrash	angle	concert
tickle	answer	compare
thank	arena	comfort
threat	anyone	condition
timid	apology	confront
timber	arcade	combat

Name: _____ Date: _____ 41

Dictionary Skills

A **dictionary** is a book that does not tell a story, but instead lists words and their meanings. A word you look up in a dictionary is called an **entry word**, and its meaning is called the **definition**. If the word has more than one meaning, its definitions will be numbered.

Look up each bold word in a dictionary and answer the questions.

1. Is a **goldfinch** a bag full of gold or a bird?

   _____

2. If you were on a **jetty**, would you be on a jet or a wall along a waterfront?

   _____

3. Is a **yak** a long-haired ox or a person who likes to talk?

   _____

4. Would you draw a **parallelogram** or do gymnastics on it?

   _____

5. Would a **narwhal** live in your aquarium or in the ocean?

   _____

6. Is a **gourd** related to you or a pumpkin?

   _____

7. Would you sit on a **davenport** or dock a boat there?

   _____

8. Would you eat a **torte** or wear it?

   _____

9. Is an **alpaca** an animal or a new type of tennis shoe?

   _____

10. Should you wear a **toga** or eat it?

    _____

Glossary

A **glossary** is a dictionary that is found at the back of a textbook. It lists words that are special to the subject of the book and gives the meanings of those words.

People and Places Glossary

Arctic—a name for the area near and around the North Pole

caribou—a deer of North America, closely related to the reindeer

cassava—a plant found in South America that provides food to the Amazon Indians

chia—a milky tea popular in the Himalayas

desert—a dry, sandy region where very few plants can grow

Himalayas—a mountain range in Asia with the highest mountains in the world

nomads—a group of people who have no permanent home but move from place to place in search of food

oasis—an area in a desert where water can be found

rain forest—a warm, rainy area where trees grow very close together; home to many insects, birds, and animals

yak—a large, long-haired, wild ox of central Asia. The yak is used in the mountains.

Use the People and Places Glossary to answer the questions.

1. You are going to read about yaks, but you do not know what a yak is. Use the glossary to find out. What is a yak? _____

    _____

2. You know that *oasis* has something to do with the desert, but you need to know its exact meaning. What do you learn about an oasis in the glossary?

    _____

    _____

3. In reading about the Amazon Indians, you see that they use the cassava plant. You look in the glossary to find out more about this plant. What do you find out?

    _____

4. *Rain forest* is in bold print in your textbook, but you cannot figure out what it means. What does the glossary say about rain forests? _____

    _____

Glossary

A **glossary** is a dictionary that is found at the back of a textbook. It lists words that are special to the subject of the book and gives the meanings of those words.

Read each set of words that are listed from a glossary. Decide what the subject of the book is. Then, circle the title of the book.

Example: alligator   crocodile   iguana   tortoise

           Felines   (*Reptiles*)   *Canines*

1. cardinal   finch   nuthatch   oriole

   Birds of the Backyard   *Birds of Prey*   *Waterbirds*

2. Little Dipper   Milky Way   North Star   Orion

   Navigation at Night   *Darkness*   *Night Sky*

3. hounds   retrievers   springers   terriers

   Choosing a Pet   *Breeds of Dogs*   *Training Your Dog*

4. air pressure   cold front   humidity   precipitation

   Dog Days of Summer   *Four Seasons*   *Weather Forecasting*

5. leopard   ocelot   panther   puma

   Wild Pets   *Big Cats*   *Circus Animals*

6. London   New York   Toronto   Tokyo

   World Cities   *World Countries*   *World Connections*

7. Spanish   German   French   Chinese

   Countries   *United Nations*   *Languages*

8. Africa   Australia   Europe   South America

   People of the World   *Continents*   *World Countries*

Name: _____ Date: _____

Glossary

A **glossary** is a dictionary that is found at the back of a textbook. It lists words that are special to the subject of the book and gives the meanings of those words.

Read each set of words that are listed from a glossary. Decide what the subject of the book is. Then, circle the title of the book.

Example: akita, golden retriever, poodle, rottweiler

(A. *Dogs as Pets*)   B. *Hunting Dogs*   C. *Canines*

1.   hickory, maple, oak, sycamore

   A. *Wildflowers*   B. *Trees in Your Backyard*   C. *Forest Lands*

2.   Lincoln Memorial, The Pentagon, U.S. Capitol, White House

   A. *Washington, D.C.*   B. *Springfield, Illinois*   C. *Seattle, Washington*

3.   Argentina, Brazil, Chile, Venezuela

   A. *North American Countries*   B. *European Countries*   C. *South American Countries*

4.   Mount Rushmore, Eiffel Tower, Taj Mahal, Stonehenge

   A. *Longitude and Latitude*   B. *Traditional Landmarks*   C. *Places on a Street Map*

5.   baseball, basketball, football, hockey

   A. *Ball Games*   B. *Winter Games*   C. *Competitive Team Sports*

6.   heart, kidneys, liver, lungs

   A. *The Respiratory System*   B. *Organs of the Body*   C. *The Nervous System*

7.   Newton, Sir Isaac; Pasteur, Louis; Salk, Jonas; Van Allen, James

   A. *Twentieth Century Inventions*   B. *American Biographies*   C. *Famous Scientists*

8.   Apache, Cherokee, Iroquois, Navajo

   A. *America's Past*   B. *Native Americans*   C. *America's European Beginnings*

9.   Amazon, Congo, Mississippi, Nile

   A. *Major World Rivers*   B. *Water Transportation*   C. *Rivers in America*

10.   Beethoven, Chopin, Mozart, Wagner

   A. *Famous Painters*   B. *Famous Musicians*   C. *Famous Composers*

Key Words

Key words can help you look up information. First, ask yourself, "What do I want to know about?" The answer should tell you the key words.

Examples: What did Thomas <u>Edison</u> invent? (Usually, when you look up a person, you should use the last name.)

Was <u>Cleopatra</u> married? (Some people are best known by their first names.)

Where did John <u>Hancock</u> sign the <u>Declaration of Independence</u>? (Sometimes, more than one key word is given.)

Underline the key words in each question.

1.   When did Neil Armstrong walk on the moon?

2.   Where is Venezuela?

3.   Are bald eagles still endangered?

4.   What scientist discovered radium and polonium?

5.   When did Amelia Earhart disappear?

6.   Bermuda is a part of which country?

7.   Where was Napoleon born?

8.   How did dinosaurs become extinct?

9.   What is the length of the largest whale ever found?

10.   What galaxy is home to Earth?

Key Words

Key words can help you look up information. First, ask yourself, "What do I want to know about?" The answer should tell you the key words.

Examples: Where was Abraham <u>Lincoln</u> born? (Usually, when you look up a person, you should use the last name.)

Who was <u>Napoleon</u>? (Some people are best known by their first names.)

Who surrendered to General Ulysses <u>Grant</u> to end the <u>U. S. Civil War</u>? (Sometimes, more than one key word is given.)

Underline the key words in each question.

1. Where is Venetian glass made?

2. Who was the 32nd United States president?

3. Why is there concern about the wolf becoming extinct?

4. What were gladiators, and when were they prominent?

5. Which breeds of dogs are good bird hunters?

6. To whom did Robert E. Lee surrender?

7. Who were the Mayans, and what happened to them?

8. How long does it take Earth to travel around the sun?

9. During what years was the American Revolutionary War fought?

10. Which states were the Confederate States during the U.S. Civil War?

11. In what habitat do flamingos live?

12. Where are the migration flyways in the United States?

13. Who were the first settlers in St. Augustine, Florida?

14. In what ways can rattlesnakes be helpful and harmful?

15. How long ago was the Iron Age, and where did people live then?

16. How many nations belong to the United Nations?

Key Words

Key words can help you look up information. First, ask yourself, "What do I want to know about?" The answer should tell you the key words.

Examples: Under what circumstances did Harry <u>Truman</u> become president of the United States? (Usually, when you look up a person, you should use the last name.)

Who was <u>Galileo</u>? (Some people are best known by their first names.)

Why did Alexander <u>Hamilton</u> and Aaron <u>Burr</u> duel? (Sometimes, more than one key word is given.)

Underline the key words in each question.

1. What war did the United States enter after an attack on Pearl Harbor?

2. In what state is Mount Rushmore located?

3. Who invented the radio and the phonograph?

4. What is ozone, and of what importance is it to the environment?

5. What kind of clothing did people wear in the late 1700s?

6. In what movie did Mickey Mouse first appear?

7. How was Harriet Tubman affiliated with the Underground Railroad?

8. In what country did croquet originate?

9. In what kind of a climate does the cactus grow best?

10. What function does the liver have in your body?

11. Which animals are endangered, and what is being done to save them?

12. What is the immigration policy of the United States?

13. What changes did the Industrial Revolution bring to America?

14. What is the history of political parties in the United States?

15. What role does chlorophyll have in the growth of plants?

16. What is the difference between a solar eclipse and a lunar eclipse?

Encyclopedias

An **encyclopedia** is a book or a set of books containing informative, factual information. On the outside of each book, or **volume**, is a letter or letters that show what topics can be found inside the book. Within the volumes, everything is alphabetized.

Write the volume number that would help you find each answer.

_____ 1. Who was the eleventh U.S. president?

_____ 2. Who was Babe Ruth?

_____ 3. Where is the capital of Argentina?

_____ 4. Where is the Red Sea located?

_____ 5. When did Hawaii become a state?

_____ 6. What does an anaconda eat?

_____ 7. What countries were involved in World War I?

_____ 8. Who invented the television?

Encyclopedia	Encyclopedia	Encyclopedia	Encyclopedia	Encyclopedia	Encyclopedia	Encyclopedia	Encyclopedia	Encyclopedia	Encyclopedia	Encyclopedia
A V. 1	B V. 2	C–Ch V. 3	Ci–Cz V. 4	D V. 5	E V. 6	F V. 7	G V. 8	H V. 9	I V. 10	J V. 11
Encyclopedia	Encyclopedia	Encyclopedia	Encyclopedia	Encyclopedia	Encyclopedia	Encyclopedia	Encyclopedia	Encyclopedia	Encyclopedia	Encyclopedia
K V. 12	L V. 13	M V. 14	N–O V. 15	P V. 16	Q–R V. 17	S–Sn V. 18	So–Sz V. 19	T V. 20	U–V V. 21	W–Z V. 22

Encyclopedias

An **encyclopedia** is a book or a set of books containing informative, factual information. On the outside of each book, or **volume**, is a letter or letters that show what topics can be found inside the book. Within the volumes, everything is alphabetized.

Write the volume number that would help you find each answer.

_____ 1. In what civilizations were mummies a part of the burial routine?

_____ 2. What countries use the euro for their money?

_____ 3. What are good uses of nuclear energy?

_____ 4. For what is John Philip Sousa best remembered?

_____ 5. What is the social life of the honeybee?

_____ 6. To whom is the Caldecott Medal given?

_____ 7. What countries practice capitalism?

_____ 8. What are the differences in the number of teeth that a six-year-old, a twelve-year-old, and an adult have?

_____ 9. For what purposes are longitude lines used?

_____ 10. What is the habitat of the raccoon?

Encyclopedia	Encyclopedia	Encyclopedia	Encyclopedia	Encyclopedia	Encyclopedia	Encyclopedia	Encyclopedia	Encyclopedia	Encyclopedia	Encyclopedia
A V. 1	B V. 2	C–Ch V. 3	Ci–Cz V. 4	D V. 5	E V. 6	F V. 7	G V. 8	H V. 9	I V. 10	J V. 11
Encyclopedia	Encyclopedia	Encyclopedia	Encyclopedia	Encyclopedia	Encyclopedia	Encyclopedia	Encyclopedia	Encyclopedia	Encyclopedia	Encyclopedia
K V. 12	L V. 13	M V. 14	N–O V. 15	P V. 16	Q–R V. 17	S–Sn V. 18	So–Sz V. 19	T V. 20	U–V V. 21	W–Z V. 22

Encyclopedias

An **encyclopedia** is a book or a set of books containing informative, factual information. On the outside of each book, or **volume**, is a letter or letters that show what topics can be found inside the book. Within the volumes, everything is alphabetized.

Write the volume numbers that would help you find each answer.

_____   1. What kind of vegetation grows in the Arctic?

_____   2. From what country do pandas come, and what do they like to eat?

_____   3. On what continent is Luxembourg located?

_____   4. Make a time line showing the history of transportation.

_____   5. What part did the Alamo play in Texas history?

_____   6. Make a list of reptiles in North America and the characteristics they share.

_____   7. What is the difference between a tornado and a hurricane?

_____   8. What did Louis Pasteur invent?

_____   9. Who was president when the U.S. negotiated the Louisiana Purchase?

_____   10. What discoveries did Magellan make?

_____   11. List England's monarchs from William the Conqueror to the present.

_____   12. Who were the Allied nations in World War II?

_____   13. What is the life cycle of salmon?

_____   14. Who were the Etruscans, and what were their accomplishments?

_____   15. When did printing begin, and how did it change culture?

Encyclopedia	Encyclopedia	Encyclopedia	Encyclopedia	Encyclopedia	Encyclopedia	Encyclopedia	Encyclopedia	Encyclopedia	Encyclopedia	Encyclopedia	Encyclopedia
A–Cee V. 1	Cef–End V. 2	Ene–Fil V. 3	Fim–Hab V. 4	Hac–Kel V. 5	Kem–Mad V. 6	Mae–Nos V. 7	Not–Par V. 8	Pas–Sab V. 9	Sac–Tad V. 10	Tae–Wal V. 11	Wam–Z V. 12

Name: _____   Date: _____

Atlas

An **atlas** is a book that includes many maps. The maps may show cities, states, provinces, countries, or the world. Sometimes, an atlas includes other facts too.

Use the map of Maryland to answer the questions.

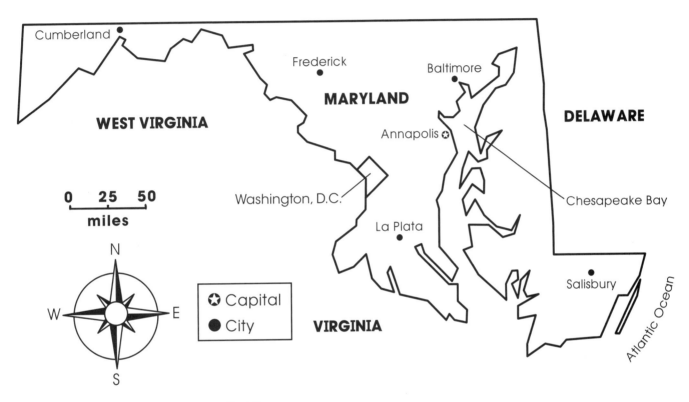

1. What is the state capital? _____
2. Where is Washington D.C. in relation to Annapolis? _____
3. Is La Plata north or south of Baltimore? _____
4. Which city is closest to the Atlantic Ocean? _____
5. What body of water divides Maryland? _____
6. Which city is located on the Eastern Shore? _____
7. Is Frederick east or west of Salisbury? _____
8. Which state is northeast of Maryland? _____
9. What ocean is nearest to Maryland? _____
10. What city is closest to West Virginia? _____

Name: _____   Date: _____

Atlas

An **atlas** is a book that has a collection of maps. The maps may show cities, states, provinces, countries, or the world. Sometimes, an atlas includes informative tables or other factual matter. Some atlases are specialized. They might include maps of the night sky, rivers, or populations.

Use the map of Illinois to answer the questions.

1. What river runs along the western side of Illinois?

   _____

2. About how many miles is it from Quincy to Danville?

   _____

3. What is the state's capital?

   _____

4. How many states border Illinois?

   _____

5. What direction do you have to travel to get from East St. Louis to Chicago?

   _____

6. What is the most southern city in Illinois?

   _____

7. What body of water is northeast of Illinois?

   _____

8. If you live in Rantoul, which bordering state would be the closest to you?

   _____

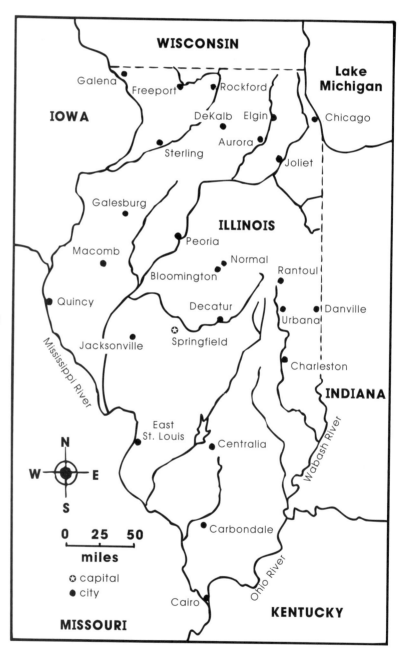

Name: _____ Date: _____

Atlas

An **atlas** is a book that has a collection of maps. The maps may show cities, states, provinces, countries, or the world. Sometimes, an atlas includes informative tables or other factual matter. Some atlases are specialized. They might include maps of the night sky, rivers, or populations.

Use the map of Missouri to answer the questions.

1. What is the state's capital? _____

2. How many states border Missouri? _____

3. Which states border Missouri on the west? _____

_____

4. Which cities have three major highways going through them? _____

_____

5. What river borders Missouri on the east? _____

6. Which city is east of the capital? _____

7. Springfield is what direction from the capital? _____

Use the number and letter pairs to identify the cities by going across from the numbers and up from the letters.

8. 2, B _____

9. 5, A _____

10. 4, C _____

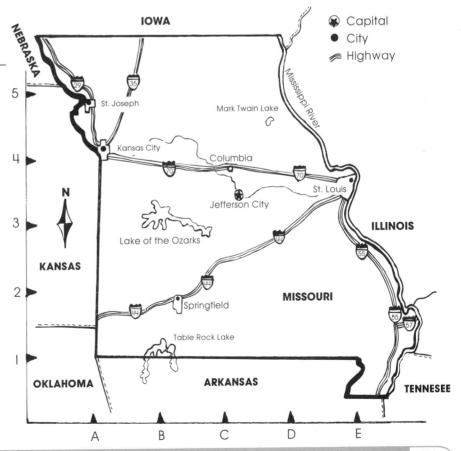

Table of Contents and Index

The **table of contents** and the **index** in a book are directories. The table of contents is found at the front of a book. It lists each chapter by its title or subject. If a book has an index, it is at the end of the book. The index lists specific names and subjects in alphabetical order and the precise page or pages where information about them can be found.

Using the table of contents and index, write the page numbers on which you would look to find the answers. If there are no listings, leave the lines blank.

	TOC	Index
1. How do you know when something tastes sour?	_____	_____
2. How many bones are in your skeleton?	_____	_____
3. What color is your blood?	_____	_____
4. How can you make yourself stronger?	_____	_____
5. How fast do nerve impulses travel?	_____	_____

Table of Contents and Index

The **table of contents** and the **index** in a book are directories. The table of contents is found at the front of a book. It lists each chapter by its title or subject. If a book has an index, it is at the end of the book. The index lists specific names and subjects in alphabetical order and the precise page or pages where information about them can be found.

Using the table of contents and index, write the page numbers on which you would look to find the answers. If there are no listings, leave the lines blank.

Table of Contents

Index

	TOC	Index
1. What is the difference between a meteor and a meteorite?	_____	_____
2. Why is Mars called the red planet?	_____	_____
3. Who invented the telescope?	_____	_____
4. How are the stars grouped to form Ursa Major?	_____	_____
5. What is the temperature of the sun?	_____	_____

Table of Contents and Index

The **table of contents** and the **index** in a book are directories. The table of contents is found at the front of a book. It lists each chapter by its title or subject. If a book has an index, it is at the end of the book. The index lists specific names and subjects in alphabetical order and the precise page or pages where information about them can be found.

Using the table of contents and index, write the page numbers on which you would look to find the answers. If there are no listings, leave the lines blank.

Table of Contents

Index

	TOC	Index
1. What is the connection between ozone and cancer cells?	_____	_____
2. What things destroy ozone in the atmosphere?	_____	_____
3. What is ozone?	_____	_____
4. What are the layers of the atmosphere?	_____	_____
5. Are there solutions to the ozone problem?	_____	_____

Name: _____ Date: _____

Choosing Reference Materials

Reference materials tell you specific information about something. There are several kinds of reference books in the library.

A. newspaper— printed daily information (news)

B. encyclopedia— a set of factual books

C. dictionary—a book of words and their meanings

D. phone book— a listing of phone numbers

E. atlas—a collection of maps

On each index card, write the letter of the material you could use to find the answer.

1. How far is it from New York, New York to Miami, Florida?	2. What does *dabble* mean?
3. Who won the baseball game last night?	4. Who was King Ludwig II of Bavaria?
5. Whom could we call to fix our piano?	6. How many types of oak trees are there?

Name: _____ Date: _____

Choosing Reference Materials

Reference materials tell you specific information about something. There are several kinds of reference books in the library.

A **dictionary** tells you what words mean. These explanations are called definitions. They also tell you how the words sound and are spelled. The words in a dictionary are listed in alphabetical order.

An **encyclopedia** tells you information about a topic. You can look up a general topic such as animals or cats. The information in an encyclopedia is listed in alphabetical order. In a set of encyclopedias, there is usually a different volume (book) for each letter of the alphabet.

An **atlas** is a book of maps. You would look here if you needed to know where something is located.

Read each line of information carefully. Write *D* if you would find the information in a dictionary, *E* if you would find it in an encyclopedia, or *A* if you would find it in an atlas.

_____ 1. information on poison oak

_____ 2. the spelling of *astronaut*

_____ 3. the location of Mexico

_____ 4. the location of the Arctic Ocean

_____ 5. information about Abraham Lincoln

_____ 6. information about the praying mantis

_____ 7. the definition of *easel*

_____ 8. the location of Saudi Arabia

_____ 9. information on Saudi Arabia

_____ 10. the meaning of *bough*

Answer the following questions.

11. If you went to the library to find out about hamsters, in which reference book would you look to find information? _____

12. If you went to the library to find out about Hawaii, in which reference book would you look to find the location of Hawaii? _____

Name: _____ Date: _____

Choosing Reference Materials

Reference materials tell you specific information about something. There are several kinds of reference books in the library. When you have to look up something, be aware of precisely what you want to know. Then, decide what source would contain the information you need.

Circle the reference material you would use to find the following information.

1. life in the Soviet Union under Joseph Stalin
   atlas   encyclopedia   dictionary   glossary

2. words in a book associated with computers: download, byte, RAM, Internet
   dictionary   encyclopedia   glossary   table of contents

3. locations of the oceans of the world
   atlas   dictionary   index   glossary

4. desert wildlife
   index   table of contents   glossary   encyclopedia

5. definitions of spelling words: breezy, eldest, grateful, merry, oriental, stackable
   glossary   index   dictionary   table of contents

6. the chapter pertaining to French artists
   index   encyclopedia   dictionary   table of contents

7. pages relating to the constellations
   index   encyclopedia   glossary   dictionary

8. distance from Indianapolis, IN, to San Diego, CA
   index   atlas   glossary   table of contents

9. definitions of words found in the second chapter of a science book
   glossary   table of contents   encyclopedia   index

10. military career of General George McClellan
    dictionary   glossary   atlas   encyclopedia

11. pages showing the rivers of Mexico
    glossary   index   atlas   dictionary

12. chapter discussing the digestive system
    index   table of contents   encyclopedia   glossary

Name: _____ Date: _____

Sequencing

Sequencing means putting events in the order in which they happened. It provides order and helps you make sense of what you read.

Our Day at Animal World

10:45–11:15	The Reptile Review
11:20–11:40	Elsie the Elephant Show
11:45–12:15	Lunch at Penguin Palace
12:30–1:00	Sea Lion Show
1:10–1:35	Birds of Prey
2:00–4:45	*The Monkey Movie*
5:00–6:00	Dinner at the Coyote Cafe
6:10–6:25	Wildcat Wackiness
6:30–7:00	Penguins on Parade

Use the schedule to answer the questions.

1. Which show is right after the Sea Lion Show? _____

2. Will you eat lunch before or after the Elephant Show? _____

3. Which shows will you see after dinner? _____

   _____

4. Which show is before the Elephant Show? _____

5. What will you be doing at 3:00? _____

6. Where will you eat lunch? _____

Sequencing

Sequencing means putting events in the order in which they happened. It provides order and helps you make sense of what you read.

The sentences about pressing flowers are out of order. Put the sentences in order by numbering them 1–9.

_____ Pansies, violets, small grass flowers, and petunias are the best flowers for pressing and should be picked when they are at their prettiest.

_____ Before you find flowers to press, make sure you have everything else you need (facial tissue, newspaper, several heavy books).

_____ Place a thick layer of newspaper over the tissue.

_____ Then, you will have to find flowers that are good for pressing.

_____ Put several heavy books on top of the newspaper.

_____ Leave the tissue, newspaper, and books this way for 24 hours.

_____ Lay the flowers flat between two layers of facial tissue.

_____ Replace the tissue and put the newspaper and books back for another 24 hours to be sure that the flowers will be dry.

_____ After 24 hours, carefully remove the books, newspaper, and tissue.

The sentences about making a floral picture are out of order. Put the sentences in order by numbering them 1–6.

_____ Cut two circles from different colors of construction paper. Make one a little larger than the other.

_____ Finally, put a ribbon through the hole and tie it in a loop so that you can hang your picture.

_____ Now, with the circles ready, use tweezers to arrange the pressed flowers and glue them into place.

_____ Next, glue the small circle on top of the larger one.

_____ Gather your materials before you begin. You will need scissors, construction paper, white glue, paper punch, tweezers, pressed flowers, and ribbon.

_____ Then, punch one hole on the outer rim of the two circles.

Sequencing

A **time line** shows dates and events in the order in which they happened.

Study the time line and complete the activities.

Oct. 4, 1957 (The USSR launched *Sputnik 1*, the first human-made satellite.)

Nov. 3, 1957 (The USSR launched *Sputnik 2*, which carried the first space traveler, a dog.)

Apr. 12, 1961 (The USSR launched *Vostok 1*, the first manned flight, with Major Yuri Gagarin.)

Feb. 20, 1962 (John Glenn, aboard *Mercury 6*, was the first American to orbit Earth.)

Oct. 16–19, 1963 (The USSR's Valentina Tereshkova, aboard *Vostok 6*, was the first woman in space.)

Mar. 18, 1965 (The USSR completed the first space walk from *Voskhod 2*.)

Dec. 21–27, 1968 (*Apollo 8* from the U.S. was the first manned flight to orbit the moon.)

July 16–24, 1969 (Neil Armstrong and Edwin Aldrin, aboard the U.S.'s *Apollo 11*, made the first moon landing.)

May 14, 1973 (The first U.S. space station was established.)

Dec. 4, 1978 (*Pioneer Venus* from the U.S. entered the orbit of Venus.)

April 12–14, 1981 (The U.S. flew the space shuttle *Columbia*, a reusable spacecraft.)

1. Number the space missions in the order in which they happened.

   _____ *Vostok 6*

   _____ *Sputnik 2*

   _____ *Columbia*

   _____ *Apollo 8*

2. Match each space explorer with the date of the mission.

   _____ July 16–24, 1969

   _____ February 20, 1962

   _____ April 12, 1961

   _____ October 16–19, 1963

   A. Yuri Gagarin
   B. Neil Armstrong
   C. Valentina Tereshkova
   D. John Glenn

3. Number the firsts in the order in which they happened.

   _____ the first U.S. space station

   _____ the first human-made satellite

   _____ the first woman in space

   _____ the first manned flight to orbit the moon

   _____ the first space walk

   _____ the first moon walk

Sequencing Events

Putting a series of events in order is called **sequencing**.

The sentences in the paragraphs are out of order. Rewrite each paragraph so that it makes sense.

Charlie had to run to catch the school bus. If he had eaten breakfast at home, he would have had a three-mile walk. The alarm did not go off in the Coles's house, and everyone overslept. When Charlie found a seat and sat down, he ate the apple that he had grabbed on his way out the door.

_____

_____

_____

_____

_____

_____

It was Field Day. Charlie was wearing a green shirt because he was on the green team. That meant that the entire school was divided into six teams: red, white, blue, green, yellow, and orange. Charlie was glad to be on the bus because today was a special day at school.

_____

_____

_____

_____

_____

_____

Sequencing Events

Putting a series of events in order is called **sequencing**.

Read the passage. Then, put the events in order by numbering them 1–8.

In October 1957, the first human-made satellite was put into orbit. It was called *Sputnik 1* and was put into space by the United States' main rival, the Union of Soviet Socialist Republics (USSR). A month later, the USSR tested the effects of space travel on living creatures by sending a dog into orbit.

The United States was humiliated at being left behind in the exploration of space. It began to accelerate its research and catch up to the Soviets. In 1958, the United States sent a satellite into orbit. In July of that year, Americans established a center for the exploration of space called the National Aeronautics and Space Administration (NASA).

In April 1961, the USSR sent a man, Yuri Gagarin, into space. A month later, Alan Shepard became the first American in space. He was followed within the year by John Glenn, who was the first American to orbit Earth. But, the USSR continued to lead the race by sending the first woman into space and landing an unmanned spacecraft intact on the moon. It was not until July 20, 1969, when Neil Armstrong, an American, walked on the moon, that the United States caught up with its main rival.

_____ The USSR sent Yuri Gagarin into space.

_____ The USSR put *Sputnik 1* into orbit.

_____ Neil Armstrong was the first person to walk on the moon.

_____ The USSR launched a dog into space.

_____ John Glenn was the first American to orbit Earth.

_____ The United States sent an unmanned satellite into orbit and established NASA.

_____ Alan Shepard was the first American to be launched into space.

_____ The USSR sent a woman into space and an unmanned spacecraft that touched down intact on the moon.

Sequencing Events

Putting a series of events in order is called **sequencing**.

Read the passage. Then, put the events in order by numbering them 1–8.

One of the better-known prehistoric peoples of the southwestern United States are the Anasazi. We do not know what the Anasazi called themselves. Anasazi is the name given to them by those who have studied prehistoric Native Americans of the Southwest.

The Anasazi most likely came to the Southwest around 100 B.C. They built their simple homes with sticks and mud in shallow caves along canyon walls. They were expert basket weavers, and therefore, this first phase is called the Early Basket Maker Period. These Anasazi existed until around 400 A.D.

The next Anasazi phase is named the Modified Basket Maker Period. These Anasazi wanted to be closer to their crops, so they built their homes in open areas near the land they farmed. Their homes were called pit houses, because they were built partially underground. During this period, the Anasazi still made baskets, but they also began making clay pots.

The Great Pueblo Period began around 1100 A.D. During this period, the Anasazi built cliff dwellings that look like today's apartment buildings. They used ladders to get into the upper stories. They could pull these ladders inside to keep enemies from entering. Sometimes, several of these cliff dwellings were built near each other to form communities. Trade with nearby tribes began during this period.

What became of the Anasazi remains a mystery. Was there a drought, warring nomadic tribes, a lack of good topsoil, or a combination? It is believed that they may have drifted into the areas that are now occupied by other pueblo dwellers of New Mexico, the Hopi, and the Zuni.

_____ The first phase is named the Early Basket Maker Period.

_____ What actually happened to the Anasazi remains a mystery.

_____ The Anasazi probably came to the Southwest around 100 B.C.

_____ The Great Pueblo Period began around 1100 A.D.

_____ The second phase is named the Modified Basket Maker Period.

_____ The homes of the last phase are similar to today's apartment buildings.

_____ They made excellent baskets.

_____ During the Modified Basket Period, the Anasazi's homes were built in open areas near the land they farmed and were partly underground.

Main Idea

The **main idea** of a story tells what the story is about. Usually, the main idea in a story or passage is stated at the beginning. There are times when it is at the end. *Aesop's Fables* are examples of this. Each fable tells a story to illustrate a lesson or moral. The end of the story wraps up, or summarizes, the lesson.

Read the summary of each fable. Circle the moral of each story.

The Hare and the Tortoise

One day, a hare was making fun of a tortoise and called him a slowpoke. That made the tortoise mad, so he challenged the hare to a race. Of course, the hare knew that he would win. When the hare got far ahead, he stopped for a rest and fell asleep. The tortoise plodded along, never stopping. When the hare woke up, he ran as fast as he could to the finish line. However, the tortoise had already crossed it.

1. A. A lazy hare is fast.

    B. Do not be a bragger.

    C. The slow turtle wins.

The Fox and the Crow

A crow sat in a tree with a piece of cheese that it had just taken from an open window. A fox who walked by saw the crow and wanted the cheese. The fox complimented the crow in many ways. The fox told the crow how nicely it sang. To prove its voice, the crow opened its mouth to sing. The cheese fell out, and the fox gobbled it up.

2. A. Do not let flattery go to your head.

    B. Listen before you sing.

    C. Eat fast so that you do not lose your dinner.

The Dog and the Bone

A dog was walking over a bridge carrying a bone. The dog looked into the stream and saw another dog carrying a bigger bone. The dog on the bridge jumped into the water because he wanted the bigger bone. But, he dropped his bone, and there was no other bone.

3. A. He lost his bone.

    B. The dog was wet.

    C. Think before you act.

Name: _____ Date: _____

Main Idea

The **main idea** of a passage tells what a story is about. The main idea may be stated in the first paragraph, or even the first several paragraphs. The remaining paragraphs have **supporting ideas** that explain who, what, where, when, why, and how about the main idea.

Read the passage. Then, follow the directions below.

The brain is an organ that controls almost everything that the human body does. It is divided into three parts. Each part controls different bodily functions. The three parts are the medulla, the cerebellum, and the cerebrum.

The medulla is located where the spinal cord enters the head. It takes care of involuntary actions. Involuntary actions do not require any decision making. They happen without any thought. Breathing, digestion, and elimination are examples of involuntary actions.

Voluntary movements demand some instruction. Brushing your teeth, dressing, and doing a somersault are examples of voluntary actions. The cerebellum is the part of the brain that controls bodily movements.

The largest part of the brain is the cerebrum. It controls voluntary mental operations, such as speaking, thinking, remembering, learning, and deciding. The cerebrum is divided into two equal parts called hemispheres. The hemispheres are covered by a layer of nerve cells called the cortex. There are many centers located in different areas of the cortex that send and receive messages. Each of the operations that the cerebrum controls is located in a different center.

Write each word or phrase in the diagram to show the main idea and its supporting ideas.

A.   involuntary actions
B.   parts of the brain
C.   cerebellum
D.   medulla
E.   cerebrum
F.   voluntary movements
G.   voluntary mental operations

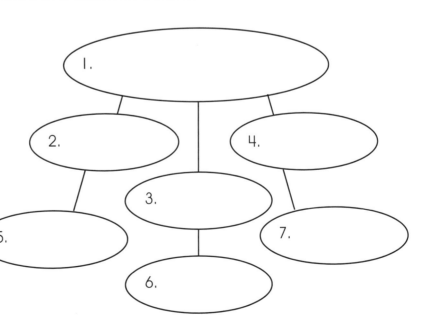

Main Idea

The **main idea** of a passage tells what a story is about. The main idea may be stated in the first paragraph, or even the first several paragraphs. The remaining paragraphs have **supporting ideas** that explain who, what, where, when, why, and how about the main idea.

Read the passage and follow directions below.

Laws are rules that we live by every day. Imagine if drivers paid no attention to stop lights, if pedestrians crossed roads wherever and whenever they wanted, or if speed limits did not exist. Traffic laws maintain safety and also protect the rights of others.

Laws are enforced by the police and the courts. Police officers make sure that the laws are obeyed, and courts enforce the laws. Judges in the courts make sure that laws are carried out fairly and "according to the law" (written rules and regular ways of punishing people who disobey the rules).

Courts in the United States have three responsibilities. First, they interpret the laws and make sure that they are followed by everyone. Second, the courts determine punishment for those who are found guilty of breaking the laws. Finally, they must protect the rights of every individual.

Laws can be changed to meet the needs of a nation. Although laws have changed over the years, the principles that govern the judicial system have not. They ensure that everyone is protected equally under the laws and has a right to a fair trial with a fitting punishment for a crime. But most importantly, these principles guarantee that every citizen has the right to practice the many freedoms specified in the U.S. Constitution.

1. What is the main idea? _____

    _____

2. Circle the supporting idea in the first paragraph.

    Laws are rules.   Pedestrians travel on foot.   Traffic laws maintain safety.

3. Circle the supporting idea in the third paragraph.

    The U.S. has a court system.   The courts must protect individual rights.

                            Punishments may differ.

4. Circle the answer to the following question. Why do we have laws?

    for the judicial system   for punishment   to protect the rights of everyone

Name: _____   Date: _____

More Main Idea

The **main idea** of a passage tells what the passage is about. The main idea of a paragraph is often stated in the first or second sentence and may be summed up in the final sentence.

Read the passage. Underline the sentence in each paragraph that tells its main idea.

One reason to classify animals is to determine which ones are related to each other. Usually, such classification is achieved by studying the skeletons and skins of the animals. Have you ever wondered to which animal you are related?

Monkeys and apes belong to a group called primates. (The word *primate* comes from a Latin word meaning first.) Monkeys and apes are primates because they have complex brains. They are the most intelligent of all animals. Human beings are also classified as primates. Monkeys and apes have large brains like us and use their front limbs as hands. Monkeys, apes, and humans can think and use tools.

Early primates probably ate insects, but they also ate leaves and fruits. The chimpanzee is the most human looking of the primates. Although it eats mostly fruits, it will eat vegetables. It has even been seen eating insects and killing and eating small animals. Chimpanzees use sticks to get honey from honeycombs or to dig out ants and termites from their nests.

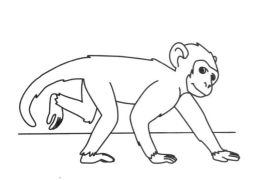 

Name: _____ Date: _____

More Main Idea

The **main idea** of a passage tells what the passage is about. The main idea of a paragraph is often stated in the first or second sentence and may be summed up in the final sentence. The main idea is supported by the sentences in the passage. These sentences are **supporting ideas**.

Read the supporting sentences and circle the main idea they support.

1. A. Farming was not always as efficient as it is today.

    B. Sometimes, disease or bad weather ruined the crops before they were ready to harvest. Therefore, when there was a good harvest, people had a reason to celebrate.

    People would be hungry if there was a poor crop.

    Today, farmers use fertilizer to grow better crops.

    Long ago, festivals were held when there was a good harvest.

2. A. They gave thanks because they had a good harvest.

    B. The crops they gathered are now part of an American Thanksgiving feast. Traditional Thanksgiving foods include turkey, cranberry sauce, and pumpkin pie.

    The Native Americans helped the settlers plant seeds.

    The first European settlers in America had a fall festival that they named Thanksgiving.

    Turkey and harvested crops are served on Thanksgiving.

3. A. Although farming has changed, the harvest is still celebrated.

    B. Different communities and countries celebrate in different ways. Some religious groups offer fruits and vegetables to the needy.

    Food is now grown in greenhouses year-round.

    Nearly all farmers today harvest their crops with machines.

    There is usually a celebration of some sort after a harvest.

More Main Idea

The **main idea** of a passage tells what the passage is about. The main idea of a passage is usually stated in the first paragraph. The main idea is supported by the sentences in the passage. These sentences are **supporting ideas**.

Read the following passage and complete the activity below.

Ancient civilizations did not have scientific information that explained the causes of earthquakes. They made up stories that reveal their lack of understanding. One belief of some of these ancient people was that Earth was carried on the backs of animals.

Some Native Americans thought that a giant sea turtle held up Earth. They believed that when the turtle moved, Earth moved. When the turtle moved more, Earth moved more, causing cracks to form on Earth's surface.

In India, it was believed that four elephants held up Earth. They stood on the back of a turtle, and the turtle, in turn, balanced on the back of a snake. If any of these animals moved, Earth would shake and cause an earthquake. The greater the movement was, the greater the earthquake was.

The ancient Greeks thought that earthquakes showed the gods' anger. A giant, named Atlas, had rebelled against the gods, so he had to hold the world on his shoulders as punishment. The Greeks believed that anytime Atlas adjusted Earth's weight on his shoulders, an earthquake followed.

Write the main idea of the passage. Then, write a supporting idea from each of the last three paragraphs.

1. _____

_____

2. _____

_____

3. _____

_____

4. _____

_____

Title and Main Idea

The title of a passage tells what the passage is mostly about. This is the first clue about the **main idea**. The main idea is usually stated in the first or second sentence. The other sentences of the passage support the main idea by telling who, what, when, where, why, and how. A summarizing sentence or paragraph is usually at the end of the passage.

Read the passage and then follow the directions at the bottom of the page.

The Rosetta Stone

The Rosetta stone was found among the ruins in Egypt a little more than 200 years ago. It unlocked the mystery that had been puzzling historians since the time of the Greeks and Romans: what did the symbols that covered the temples and tombs of ancient Egypt mean? The Rosetta stone had been carved for people to read around 196 B.C. It was named after the place where it was found, called Rosetta.

The Rosetta stone tells about young King Ptolemy V of Egypt. He had been king for nine years and had passed laws giving more money to the priests. In return, the priests had decided to build statues of him in all of the temples and to worship the statues three times a day.

There are three different kinds of writing on the stone. The writing on the top part of the stone is lines of small pictures, called hieroglyphics. Hieroglyphics were often carved on walls or on slabs of stone. The Egyptian priests were the ones who used hieroglyphics. The second script on the stone is now known as demotic script. *Demotic* means "popular." It was used by the Greeks in their everyday writing, like in letters. The third section at the bottom of the stone is written in Greek. By 196 B.C., a Greek family called the Ptolemies had been ruling Egypt for over 100 years. Because of this, the Greek alphabet and language, along with Egyptian writing, were being used in Egypt.

1. Write the main idea of the first paragraph. _____
    _____

2. Write the main idea of the second paragraph._____
    _____

3. Write the main idea of the third paragraph._____
    _____

4. Write the main idea of the passage. _____
    _____

Title and Main Idea

The **main idea** identifies the main point (or points) in a story. The main idea in a paragraph is often stated in the first or second sentence and may be summed up in the final sentence. A title also tells what a story or passage is mostly about.

Circle the title and main idea of each paragraph.

1.   The ancient Egyptians used a reed, called papyrus, to make paper. They cut the stem into thin slices. They laid some pieces lengthwise and placed others across them. Next, they moistened the layers with water, put a heavy weight on the layers to press them together, and dried them. When the layers were dry, they stuck together in a sheet. The Egyptians rubbed the dried sheet until it was smooth and ready to write on. Sometimes, sheets were joined together to make long scrolls.

How Papyrus Was Made   How Paper Was Made

Definition of Papyrus   About Ancient Egypt

2.   In ancient times, only a few people knew how to write. Most people who needed something written had to ask a scribe to write for them. A scribe was someone who could write.

Ancient Times   Writing in Ancient Egypt

Scribes   Illiterate People in Ancient Times

3.   Pyramids are large structures with square bases and four triangular sides that come to a point at the top. They were built by the ancient Egyptians as tombs in which the bodies of their kings and queens were placed. Before the bodies were placed in the tombs, they were mummified. Then, they were placed in the tombs with personal and household items. The Egyptians hoped to hide and preserve the bodies and to protect their souls so that they could live forever. The remains of several pyramids can still be found in Egypt, but the tombs are empty. Grave robbers looted the graves.

Burying the Dead in Ancient Egypt   How Pyramids Were Built

Use of Pyramids in Ancient Egypt   Remains of the Pyramids

Title and Main Idea

The title of a passage tells what the passage is mostly about. This is the first clue about the **main idea**. The main idea is usually stated in the first or second sentence. The other sentences of the passage support the main idea by telling <u>who</u>, <u>what</u>, <u>when</u>, <u>where</u>, <u>why</u>, and <u>how</u>. A summarizing sentence or paragraph is usually at the end of the passage.

Read the paragraph and then follow the directions.

_____

   When the United States Constitution was written in 1787, it established a government in which power was split between three branches: legislative, executive, and judicial. This kept any one branch from having more power than another. The legislative branch consists of the Congress—the House of Representatives and the Senate. Members of this branch are elected by their individual states. Congress makes the laws of the nation. The executive branch is headed by the president and is responsible for enforcing the laws of the nation. The Supreme Court of the judicial branch is in charge of the federal court system. It also acts as a referee and makes sure that all laws and actions of the government follow the principles set forth in the Constitution. Although changes have been made to the Constitution over the past 200-plus years, the three branches of government remain as originally written.

1. Write a title on the line above the paragraph.

2. Underline the sentence that expresses the main idea.

3. Circle a supporting sentence. Does it tell who, what, when, where, why, or how about the main idea? _____

4. Write the summarizing sentence. _____

_____

_____

_____

Topic Sentences

Longer passages may be written in paragraphs that each tell about something different. In this case, the title should be about the entire passage. Each paragraph will have a **topic sentence** that tells about its main idea.

Read the passage. Then, answer the questions below.

Lobsters are saltwater animals belonging to a group called crustaceans. A lobster has a hard outer shell and five sets of legs. The first set of legs are known as claws. One is usually used for crushing and the other for biting. The female lobster lays thousands of eggs, and the tiny young drift and swim for three to five weeks before settling on the bottom of the ocean.

Crayfish are freshwater versions of their crustacean cousins called lobsters. Crawfish, as they are also called, may be as short as two inches (five centimeters) in length. Like their cousins, crayfish have large front claws that are actually one of five sets of legs. Crayfish are found around the world, except in Africa and Antarctica, in freshwater rivers and streams.

1. A good title for this passage would be:

   A.   River Animals

   B.   Lobsters

   C.   Cousins with Claws

2. The topic sentence of the first paragraph is:

   A.   The first set of legs are known as claws.

   B.   A lobster has a hard outer shell and five sets of legs.

   C.   Lobsters are saltwater animals belonging to a group called crustaceans.

3. The topic sentence of the second paragraph is:

   A.   Crawfish, as they are also called, may be as short as two inches (five centimeters) in length.

   B.   Crayfish are freshwater versions of their crustacean cousins called lobsters.

   C.   Crayfish are found in freshwater rivers and streams.

Topic Sentences

Longer passages may be written in paragraphs that each tell about something different. In this case, the title should be about the entire passage. Each paragraph will have a **topic sentence** that tells about its main idea.

Underline the topic sentence in each paragraph.

1.   Minnie Watson had simply had enough aggravation from her old car. It had been acting up terribly, and Minnie decided that it was time to buy a new car. She realized quickly that it was not going to be easy to replace the one that she had driven for almost 60 years.

2.   When Crystal climbed aboard the sleigh, she had no idea how special it was. Crystal soon learned that the sleigh would take her anywhere in the world. Not only that, but it would also go backward or forward in time. She could not wait for all of the adventures that she would have.

3.   Tom was tall and strong. He looked like one of those people who was not afraid of anything. Actually, Tom was afraid of more things than anyone would believe. He got nervous when he saw spiders and bugs. He was scared of dogs and thunderstorms. Tom was even afraid of the dark!

4.   There are many breeds of cattle. There are Brown Swiss and Holstein cows. There are Guernsey and black Angus cows. Some people prefer white-faced Herefords or the large white Charolais cows. Two unusual breeds are the Red Poll and the Shorthorn cows.

5.   Hugo is a hippopotamus who eats all day long. Ten times a day, the zookeeper dumps a huge wheelbarrow full of sugarcane and corn into Hugo's cage. He is usually finished with that in about 15 minutes and is howling for more. The zookeeper knows that the only way to keep Hugo happy and quiet is to keep his 10-foot-long stomach full!

6.   Jeremy kept thinking about fresh berry pie as he worked. His arms and legs were scratched from the branches and thorns. He did not especially like the bugs, and his arms were getting very tired. The sun was quite hot, and Jeremy was beginning to itch all over. Picking blackberries was really hard work, but Jeremy knew that it would be worth it when he had his piece of pie!

Topic Sentences

A **topic sentence** is a sentence that tells the main idea of a paragraph.

Write the letter for the main idea of each paragraph.

_____ 1. Gary and Fritz had been writing to each other for four years. Gary lived in Indiana, and Fritz lived in West Germany. Gary looked forward to Fritz's letters. Fritz usually sent at least one picture, and sometimes, he sent extra German stamps for Gary's collection. Gary and Fritz both hope that they can meet someday. They feel as if they know each other already.

        A. pictures from Germany

        B. Gary's German pen pal

        C. Gary's friend

_____ 2. Mary has been blind all of her life. She has gone to special schools to learn to do things for herself. Her best friend Katy is not blind. Mary and Katy help each other. Mary is trying to teach Katy to read braille. It is a special system of raised dots that lets Mary read the page. Katy is not doing very well at all. Katy says that it is hard for her to "see" the letters with her fingers.

        A. learning to read

        B. problems of being blind

        C. a special friendship

_____ 3. It is September. It is the night of the first football game of the year. Everyone at Kidwell School is excited. Most excited of all is Cliff. This is the very first night that he has ever marched with the band. He holds his clarinet nervously. As the director's white glove raises up, Cliff's heart skips a beat. He has dreamed of this moment, and it is finally here. He is a member of the marching band at last!

        A. Cliff's first night as a band member

        B. excitement on the night of the first game

        C. Cliff and his friends at the football game

_____ 4. There were so many different frames. Some were very large, and some were very small. Some were simple, and some were fancy. Carol liked every pair she tried on. Her favorite pair looked like blue ovals. They were pretty and looked nice on her too.

        A. buying a painting

        B. choosing eyeglasses

        C. Carol goes shopping

Reading for Details

Some details are harder to find because they are hidden as descriptive words (adjectives and adverbs). When you are **reading for details**, pay close attention to the descriptive words.

Read the passage and complete the puzzle.

Mark Spitz is an American swimmer who set an Olympic record when he won seven gold medals at the 1972 Summer Olympics in Germany. Mark had been swimming races since he was eight years old. By his late teens, he had already broken three world records in the freestyle and butterfly races. At the 1968 Summer Olympics in Mexico, Mark hoped to win the gold medal, but he did not swim his best. He finished second in the butterfly and third in the freestyle. With heavy training, Mark Spitz came to the 1972 Olympics ready to swim his best. And, did he ever!

Across

3. What country did Mark represent?
4. How old was Mark when he began swimming races?
6. Where were the Olympics held when Mark did not swim his best?
7. How many gold medals did Mark win in 1972?

Down

1. Which stroke was Mark's best at the Olympics in Mexico?
2. Where were the Olympics held when Mark won seven gold medals?
5. How many world records did Mark set as a teenager?

Name: _____   Date: _____

Reading for Details

Some details are harder to find because they are hidden as descriptive words (adjectives and adverbs). When you are **reading for details**, pay close attention to the descriptive words.

Read the information. Then, complete the chart.

Mollusks belong to a large family of invertebrate animals. Animals that belong to this group usually have soft, one-sectioned bodies that are covered by hard shells. A person walking on a beach might find several of their discarded shells. Animals once lived in these seashells.

Biologists divide mollusks into seven groups called classes, but only some of the mollusks have hard protective shells. Gastropoda is one class of mollusks. Most often, a gastropod has a single, coiled shell. Included in this class are limpets, slugs, snails, and whelks. They can be found on the beaches of the Atlantic and Pacific Oceans in North America.

Bivalves is another large class of mollusks. The shell of a bivalve is actually two shells hinged together at one end or along one side. The animals that call these shells home include clams, oysters, mussels, and scallops. They too, can be found on both coasts of North America.

A third class of mollusks are chitons. A chiton's body is covered by eight shell plates that look something like a turtle's shell. Merten's chiton, northern red chiton, and mossy mopalia are all included in this class. Chitons generally live in shallow rock pools. They can be found along the Pacific Ocean from Alaska to Mexico.

	Gastropods	**Bivalves**	**Chitons**
What do their shells look like?			
Where can they be found?			
List mollusks included in each class.			

Reading for Details

Some details are harder to find because they are hidden as descriptive words (adjectives and adverbs). When you are **reading for details**, pay close attention to the descriptive words.

Read the summary of *Shiloh* by Phyllis Reynolds Naylor (Aladdin, 2000). Use details from the summary to complete the puzzle. The bold spaces will tell you what award this book received.

In *Shiloh*, an award-winning book, 11-year-old Marty Preston tells about what happens when a dog follows him home. Marty lives with his parents and two sisters, Becky and Dara Lynn, in the hills above Friendly. Friendly is a small town in West Virginia near Sisterville. On a Sunday afternoon, after a big dinner of rabbit and sweet potatoes, Marty goes for a walk along the river. During his walk, Marty spies a short-haired dog. The dog, a beagle with black and brown spots, does not make a sound as he watches and follows Marty. From the dog's behavior, Marty suspects that the dog has been mistreated. Since he found the dog near the old Shiloh schoolhouse, Marty calls the dog Shiloh. Marty soon discovers that Shiloh belongs to mean Judd Travers. After returning Shiloh to Judd, Marty contemplates how he can earn enough money to buy the dog. Before Marty can solve this problem, he is faced with a difficult decision.

1. In what town does Marty live?

2. How old is Marty?

3. What kind of potatoes does the family eat on Sunday?

4. What kind of meat do they eat?

5. What kind of dog is Shiloh?

6. Write the last name of Shiloh's owner.

7. Name one of Marty's sisters.

8. What adjective is used to describe Judd Travers?

9. What is Marty's last name?

10. What day does Marty find Shiloh?

11. Who tells the story?

12. Marty finds the dog by what schoolhouse?

Supporting Details

The **supporting details** are the parts of a paragraph that tell more about the topic sentence. They describe the main idea in more detail.

Example: Jeffrey was having a great day until his mom told him that he had to share his pet snake with his sister. He knew that <u>Lana would scream and scare his new best friend</u>. Besides, <u>Lana had been playing dress-up, and she smelled like a perfume bottle</u>. No pet snake should have to smell like that.

Circle the topic sentence and underline two supporting details in each paragraph.

1.   Some people like the fire department across the street from our neighborhood, and some people do not. My mom and dad think that it is great, because they know that help could reach us within minutes. Nan's parents do not like it because of all of the noise the sirens make. I guess that I can see both sides.

2.   Every evening, Gabriel and his dad look forward to feeding the deer in their backyard. Gabriel carries the dried corn from the garage to the edge of the woods. He and his dad spread the corn. Then, they hide behind the edge of the house to watch. Each evening, the same four female deer come to feed. Maybe someday they will have a newcomer!

3.   Alley worked hard to finish all of her projects at summer camp. She made a tie-dyed shirt in shades of blue and purple, glued eyes onto her lion's mask, and carefully formed a monkey out of clay. Now, it was time for her favorite camp "project"—lunch!

4.   Tuesdays are busy for Gabriella. She gets up early for swim practice, which starts at 7:30. Then, her mom drops her off just as the morning bell rings. After the bus brings her home, Gabriella grabs a quick snack before she leaves for dance lessons. Gabriella says that she loves all of her activities, but she always eats a great dinner and goes to bed early on Tuesday nights!

Supporting Details

> The **supporting details** are the parts of a paragraph that tell more about the topic sentence. They describe the main idea in more detail.

Circle the topic sentence and underline two supporting details in each paragraph.

1. The first Englishman to sail around the world was Sir Francis Drake. Drake left on his ship, the *Pelican*, from Plymouth, England, on December 13, 1577, to travel around the world. Four other ships and 160 men began this famous voyage with him. Drake renamed his ship the *Golden Hind* during the voyage. He returned to Plymouth on September 26, 1580. The voyage made him a national hero.

2. Each class had selected four students to represent them in the geography bee. Kate was excited that she had been chosen. The contest would include questions about North and South America. Kate spent most of her time studying the countries in South America. She already knew the names and capitals of the provinces and territories in Canada. Her mom and dad prepared questions to challenge her. When the day of the bee came, Kate knew that she was ready.

3. The Statue of Liberty was a gift of friendship from France to the United States. The statue is often called Lady Liberty. Lady Liberty had to be taken apart and packed into 214 crates to travel to the United States. It was put back together in 1886. The statue is recognized as a symbol of freedom to people around the world.

4. The Vikings lived in Scandinavia from about 700 to 1100. They were fearless warriors and also skilled boat builders and sailors. They sailed their wooden longships with square sails and oars on their bold, ruthless raids in Europe. They also crossed the Atlantic Ocean to settle in Iceland and Greenland. It is thought that they landed in North America around the year 1000. In addition to being such fierce warriors, some were farmers, traders, and artists.

Supporting Details

The **supporting details** are the parts of a paragraph that tell more about the topic sentence. They describe the main idea in more detail.

Read the passage. Circle the topic sentence in each paragraph. Then, write two supporting details from each paragraph.

Pike's Peak is the name given to one of the mountains located in the Rocky Mountains of Colorado. It is not the highest peak in the state, but it is well-known for its amazing view at the top. When visiting, you can climb the mountain by horseback, cog railway, or car. Pike's Peak was named after the American explorer who discovered it in 1806.

The Royal Gorge is a deep canyon that was created by the snow and rain that run off the Rocky Mountains and into rivers. The Arkansas River runs through the bottom of the canyon, which is about 1,000 feet (305 meters) deep. Visitors can enjoy an awesome view from the suspension bridge that crosses the canyon.

Paragraph 1

Supporting Detail: _____

_____

Supporting Detail: _____

_____

Paragraph 2

Supporting Detail: _____

_____

Supporting Detail: _____

_____

Following Directions

Directions help the reader do something or get somewhere. They should be read one at a time and followed exactly in order. It may be easy to lose your place or skip important parts. To prevent this, be sure to check off the directions as you complete them.

Look at the map and follow the directions.

1. Write *B* at the northeast corner of Elm Avenue and Second Street.
2. Write *X* halfway between First Street and Flag Street on Pine Avenue.
3. Draw a circle around the intersection of Beech Avenue and Third Street.
4. Write *H* at the southwest corner of Lewis Lane and Pine Avenue.
5. Draw a flower where Elm Avenue intersects First Street.
6. Draw a line from location X to the third cross street to the east and continue the line one block north.
7. Draw a house south of Pine Avenue and east of Second Street.
8. Write *SS* where Short Street intersects Maple Avenue.
9. Write *R* at the northwest corner of Oak Avenue and Elm Avenue.

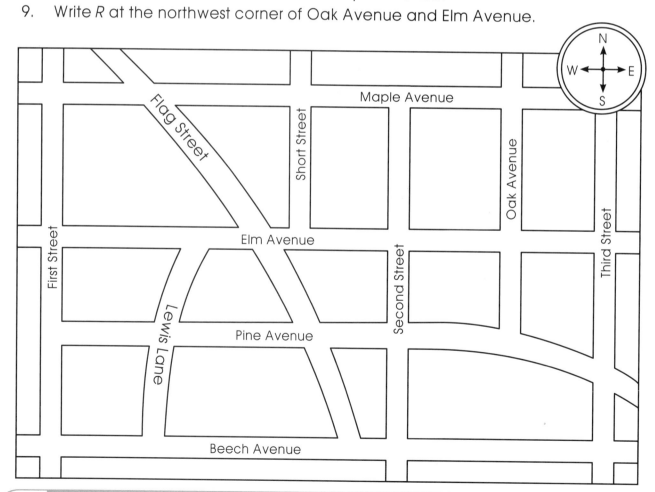

Following Directions

Directions help the reader do something or get somewhere. They should be read one at a time and followed exactly in order. It may be easy to lose your place or skip important parts. To prevent this, be sure to check off the directions as you complete them.

Read the recipe. Then, put the steps for making baking powder biscuits in order by numbering them 1–11.

Baking Powder Biscuits

2 cups all-purpose flour

1 tablespoon baking powder

1/2 teaspoon salt

5 tablespoons cold, unsalted butter or margarine, divided

2/3 cup milk

Preheat oven to 450°F. Put flour, baking powder, and salt in a large bowl and mix well. Add butter and cut it in with a fork. Add milk and stir with the fork until a soft dough forms.

Turn dough out onto a lightly floured board and knead it about 15 times. Roll dough into a circle about 1/2- to 3/4- inch thick. Cut out biscuits with a 2-inch biscuit cutter. Press the scraps together, roll out, and cut some more biscuits. Place biscuits with sides touching on an ungreased cookie sheet.

Bake 12 to 14 minutes until golden brown. Put a cotton dish towel on a wire cooling rack. Use a spatula to put the hot biscuits on the towel. Fold the towel loosely over them. Cool at least 30 minutes for the best flavor.

_____ Put flour, baking powder, and salt into a large bowl and mix well.

_____ Put dough on a floured board and knead it about 15 times.

_____ Preheat oven to 450°F.

_____ Add milk and stir with the fork until a soft dough forms.

_____ Place biscuits with sides touching on an ungreased cookie sheet.

_____ Roll dough into a 1/2- to 3/4- inch thick circle and cut out biscuits with a 2-inch biscuit cutter.

_____ Bake 12 to 14 minutes until golden brown.

_____ Press scraps together, roll out, and cut some more biscuits.

_____ Add butter and cut it in with a fork.

_____ Let biscuits stand wrapped in a towel at least 30 minutes.

_____ Use a spatula to put the hot biscuits on a towel on a cooling rack.

Name: _____   Date: _____

Following Directions

Directions are often sequenced steps that help you do something or get somewhere. Directions should be read one at a time and followed exactly.

There are several appliances in your house that you use frequently. But, you probably rarely consider what you do to make them work. Imagine that you have rented your house to someone and you need to leave directions about how to use the appliances. Put the directions in order by numbering them.

1. How to Use the Washing Machine

_____   Next, determine the size of your load and set the knob to small, medium, or large.

_____   Gently lay the dirty laundry around the center agitator.

_____   Depending on the size of your load, pour one-quarter to one-half of a cup of liquid detergent onto the clothes.

_____   Set the type of wash (regular, permanent press, or delicate) for the machine, close the lid, and pull out the knob to start the machine.

2. How to Use the DVD Player

_____   Press PLAY (>).

_____   To get the DVD out, press OPEN/CLOSE.

_____   Press OPEN/CLOSE, and the power will come on automatically.

_____   Insert the DVD, and press OPEN/CLOSE.

_____   When you are finished watching the DVD, press STOP.

3. How to Set Up and Use the Answering Machine

_____   Next, hold down the day button to set the day and stop on the correct day.

_____   Once the time and day are set, record your greeting by pressing the announce button and speaking after the tone.

_____   After listening to the message, press the erase button.

_____   To listen to messages, press the review button.

_____   First, set the time by pressing the hour button and stopping at the correct hour. Press the minute button and stop it at the correct minute.

Name: _____ Date: _____

Finding the Facts

When you find the **facts** of a passage, you can respond to specific questions with precise answers.

Read the passage and circle the facts that complete the sentences.

Rattlesnakes are poisonous reptiles whose home is anywhere from southern Canada in North America to Argentina in South America. There are 31 species of rattlesnakes. A large majority of them live in the southwestern United States and in Mexico.

A rattlesnake has excellent eyesight and a great sense of smell. Its forked tongue senses a combination of smells and tastes. A rattlesnake has no external ears, so it cannot receive outside sounds. Its scales and bones enable it to detect ground vibrations.

The rattlesnake has two long teeth called fangs. The fangs inject a bitten animal with the snake's poison, called venom. Rattlesnakes hunt and eat rodents, small birds, lizards, and frogs. Because snakes digest food slowly, a rattlesnake may not hunt for several days.

The rattlesnake's rattle is probably its best-known feature. It is a series of interlocking segments that vibrate whenever the tail shakes. When you hear its rattle, you do not want to go any closer.

1. Rattlesnakes are _____ and _____.

          good pets   reptiles   poisonous

2. Rattlesnakes have _____ and _____.

          fangs   different colors   no ears

3. Rattlesnakes eat _____ and _____.

          rodents   small birds   humans

4. Rattlesnakes live in _____ and _____.

          Mexico   South America   Alaska

5. Rattlesnakes can _____ and _____.

          talk   see   smell

Finding the Facts

When you find the **facts** of a passage, you can respond to specific questions with precise answers.

Read the passage. Then, find the facts to answer the questions.

The pioneers followed several different routes on their way west. One route went through the Cumberland Gap, a natural pass in the Appalachian Mountains that ended near where Kentucky, Tennessee, and Virginia meet. In 1775, several woodsmen led by Daniel Boone cut the Wilderness Road, another route. And, pioneers from New England traveled across New York on the Mohawk Trail.

The first groups of settlers crossed the Appalachian Mountains in the late 1700s and early 1800s by following these early trails. Usually, pioneer families joined several others who wanted to move west. Some pioneers traveled on foot carrying only a rifle, an ax, and a few supplies, but most went by wagon. Either way, they did not take many belongings, especially anything that could be made along the way. They hunted, fished, and used dried staples that they carried with them.

The pioneers were able to travel only short distances every day, so most trips took several weeks.

1. Who followed the Mohawk Trail? _____

2. Where did the trail that went through the Cumberland Gap end? _____

   _____

3. How did the pioneers get food? _____

   _____

4. Who was responsible for the Wilderness Road? _____

5. When did the first groups of settlers head west? _____

6. Which trail crossed New York? _____

7. How did the pioneers travel? _____

8. How long did most trips take? _____

Finding the Facts

When you find the **facts** of a passage, you can respond to specific questions with precise answers.

Read the passage and circle the fact that completes each sentence below.

Originally, the number of justices who sat on the U.S. Supreme Court varied from six to ten. But from 1869 to this day, the Court has had nine justices: one chief justice and eight associate justices.

The Court may consider 5,000 cases, but usually, only several hundred cases come before it. The cases are either of national importance or they challenge a law based on constitutional grounds.

Every case that comes before the Court is given the name of the parties involved. If Mr. Jones is suing the U.S. government, the case is called Jones v. the U.S. Government. When the justices decide a case, it becomes a precedent, which means that the decision becomes the basis of future rulings.

All U.S. Supreme Court justices are appointed by the president and approved by the Senate. Supreme Court justices may hold their seats until they die. If a justice acts improperly or is corrupt, the justice may be impeached and removed from the Court.

The Court's most important duty is to maintain the laws as laid out in the Constitution. The authors of the U.S. Constitution could not have known what life would be like in the 21st century. Therefore, it is up to the Court to make adjustments as they relate to every individual's constitutional rights.

1. Justices may be _____ from the Court if they act improperly.
    A. accused and barred   B. blamed and banned
    C. fired   D. impeached and removed

2. The Court hears _____ cases in a year.
    A. 5,000   B. 100
    C. several hundred   D. about 100

3. A case decided by the Court becomes the _____ of future rulings.
    A. law   B. basis
    C. impression   D. point

4. Originally, there were _____ justices on the Court.
    A. six to ten   B. seven to nine
    C. ten   D. nine

Reading a Chart

Charts and **tables** are helpful in organizing information. To read a chart, match the given information from the top and side to find new information in the boxes.

Subjects	Monday	Tuesday	Wednesday	Thursday	Friday
Reading	unit 1	unit 2	unit 3	unit 4	review
Writing	brainstorm	rough draft	revise	edit	final draft
Math	pp. 21–22	pp. 23–24	pp. 25–26	pp. 27–30	line graph
Science	plant seeds		record results		record results
S. Studies		finish map		time line	

Use the information from the chart to answer the questions.

1. What assignment is due on Wednesday in science? _____

2. What assignment is due on Thursday in writing? _____

3. On what day is the time line due in social studies? _____

4. In what subject do pages 27–30 need to be read by Thursday? _____

5. What assignment is due on Monday in social studies? _____

6. On what day is unit 2 due in reading? _____

7. On what day is the line graph due in math? _____

8. What assignment is due on Tuesday in writing? _____

Due Tuesday PP. 23-24

Due Friday Record Results

Due Wednesday Math

Due Monday Unit 1

Reading a Chart

Charts and **tables** are helpful in organizing information. To read a chart, match the given information from the top and side to find new information in the boxes.

Dinosaurs lived long ago—about 60 million years ago. Today, all that is left of them are their fossils, bones, and footprints. But, what does 60 million years mean to us? A geologic time scale was developed by scientists that illustrates the periods in Earth's history. It can help those of us living today gain some perspective about the time involved in the development of life on Earth.

Read the chart and answer the questions.

1. Earth's history is divided into how many major eras? _____

2. What are the eras' names?

   _____

   _____

   _____

   _____

3. In which era did the dinosaurs exist?

   _____

4. Into how many periods is the Mesozoic era divided?

   _____

5. What are the Mesozoic periods' names?

   _____

   _____

   _____

6. In which era do you live?

   _____

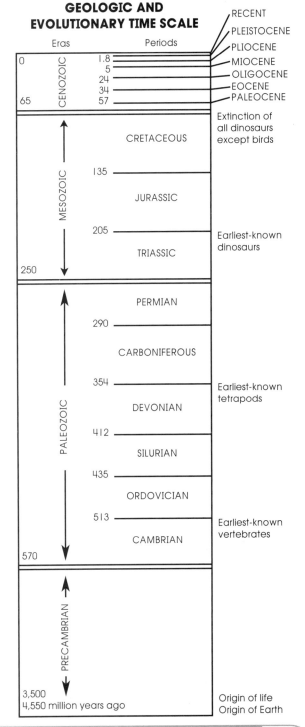

GEOLOGIC AND EVOLUTIONARY TIME SCALE

Name: _____ Date: _____

Charts and **tables** are helpful in organizing information. To read a chart, match the given information from the top and side to find new information in the boxes.

Use the chart to answer the questions.

	Area (in sq. mi.)	Highest Mountain (in feet)	Lowest Point (feet below sea level)	Longest River (in miles)
Africa	11,700,000	Kilimanjaro (19,340)	Lake Assal (512)	Nile (4,145)
Antarctica	5,400,000	Vinson Massif (16,864)	not known	no rivers
Asia	17,200,000	Mount Everest (29,028)	Dead Sea (1,312)	Yangtze (3,915)
Australia	3,071,000	Mount Kosciusko (7,310)	Lake Eyre (52)	Murray-Darling (2,310)
Europe	3,580,000	Elbrus (18,510)	Caspian Sea (92)	Volga (2,194)
North America	9,400,000	Mount McKinley (20,320)	Death Valley (282)	Missouri (2,540)
South America	6,900,000	Aconcagua (22,834)	Valdes Peninsula (131)	Amazon (4,000)

1. Which continent has the highest mountain and the lowest point?

   _____

2. What are the two longest rivers? _____

3. Which continents are about the same size? _____

4. Which continent has the shortest mountain and the highest lowest point?

   _____

5. List the mountains that are greater than 20,000 feet high.

   _____

Context Clues

At times you may not recognize a word in a sentence or know its meaning, but **context clues** can help to figure it out. One context clue is a word's part of speech.

Example: The carpet's colors <u>harmonize</u> with those of the walls and furniture. (Decide what part of speech the underlined word is, what function it has in the sentence, and what it actually means.)

Another context clue is the other words in the sentence.

Example: The team was <u>forlorn</u> after losing the game. (The other words tell you that the team was sad.)

Use context clues to complete each sentence with one of the words in parentheses.

1. _____

   is one of Tom's favorite subjects. (Astronaut, Astronomy, Atmosphere)

2. He _____ liked to follow the movement of the stars.

   (especially, establish, exceptionally)

3. Tom was delighted when his family gave him a _____
   for his birthday. (telegram, telephoned, telescope)

4. Part of his birthday present was to go camping with his father in a park
   where _____ were good
   for stargazing. (constellations, conditions, conjunctions)

5. When the night came for Tom to go to the park, he took the necessary
   equipment with which to make his _____.
   (observes, orbits, observations)

6. Tom saw several _____, including Orion and the dippers.

   (consultants, constellations, confirmations)

7. He drew pictures of what he saw and recorded their positions using
   a _____. (compass, confess, congress)

8. He had a wonderful time and asked if his father would take him on another
   _____ to observe the stars.

   (explore, expedition, experience)

Context Clues

Context clues can help you figure out a word's meaning. A word's part of speech and the other words in the sentence are examples of context clues.

Read the passage. Write each bold word next to its definition below.

The Space Age began in 1957 when the Union of Soviet Socialist Republics (USSR) **launched** the first satellite named *Sputnik 1*. Though the satellite was very small, the importance of its mission **transformed** how the world was able to look at space. *Sputnik 1* was the first object to go beyond Earth's **atmosphere**. Since then, thousands of satellites have been launched, mostly by the **former** USSR and the United States. Today, the satellites are much larger and heavier. Some weigh several tons, and their **payloads** have a purpose related to the design of each satellite's **mission**. Today's satellites are designed to perform different tasks, including exploring Earth and space, observing the weather, improving communications, and assisting the military.

Until the Space Age, there were **theories** about space that could not be proven. They could only be **evaluated** from observations and using instruments on the ground. The atmosphere that surrounds Earth **distorts** the way the stars really look because of the substances within the atmosphere. By putting satellites beyond Earth's atmosphere, scientists can get a better picture of distant stars and perhaps the **universe**.

1. the layers of gases surrounding a planet _____

2. initiated; released _____

3. determined; tested _____

4. a specific task _____

5. changed _____

6. twists the normal shape _____

7. before in time _____

8. beliefs; analyses of a set of facts _____

9. everything in a space system _____

10. loads carried by a satellite necessary for the flight _____

Context Clues

Context clues can help you figure out a word's meaning. A word's part of speech and the other words in the sentence are examples of context clues.

Read the passage. Then, write each bold word next to its definition below.

The rocky land of the northern forests in North America was never good for farming. Without fish and game, the early **natives** would have starved. Their lives were **contingent** on the animals they hunted.

In order to survive, the early Native Americans of the North American forests played games that **incorporated** the skills they needed to be successful in their **culture**. They needed to be able to judge distances, pick up clues and signs from their environment, and conceal themselves from the animals they hunted. In one of the games the Native Americans played, the men threw axes. In another, they took turns throwing spears or sticks into a hoop on the ground. Such games improved the players' **accuracy**.

Moose and caribou were very important to the tribes. Moose usually lived and traveled by themselves. Caribou migrated in herds covering a large territory each season. The Native Americans **stalked** the moose from one **range** to another, but when hunting caribou, they would wait for them at a place along the caribou's trails.

Weirs, nets, traps, hooks, and spears were used to catch fish. Whitefish and jackfish were caught in lakes, and Arctic grayling and trout were caught in rivers. The Native Americans fished from the shore or in canoes in summer and through holes cut in the ice in winter.

After the ice melted, the traps were set. Sometimes, the Native Americans would discover a bear still hibernating in its den. Such a kill would feed the camp for a few days. Sometimes, when meat was scarce, the Native Americans would eat rabbit, mink, or wolverine. When hunting became poor, they lived on dried meat and fish and on pemmican, a mixture of dried meat and animal fat.

1. open area on which animals roam _____
2. combined into one body _____
3. original inhabitants _____
4. dependent upon _____
5. pursued prey _____
6. quality of being exact _____
7. enclosures set in a waterway for catching fish _____
8. one's social group _____

Drawing Conclusions

When you **draw conclusions**, you consider the information you have and come up with answers based on that information. The answers may not have been stated directly in what you read.

Example: We saw one of the zookeepers training an animal, who swims and lives on the rocks in one of the zoo's ponds, to balance a ball on its nose. Was it a tiger, monkey, giraffe, or seal? (It would not be a tiger, monkey, or giraffe, because they do not swim or live in a zoo pond. So, the answer would be seal.)

Circle the animal that fits each description. Then, write the clues that helped you choose that animal.

1.   The zoo had a high wall around it. As we drove past it on our way to the entrance, we could see one of the animal's heads as it stretched to eat leaves from the trees.

    ape   walrus   wolf   giraffe

    What clues made you select this animal? _____

    _____

    _____

2.   As we entered the zoo, several animals in a large wire cage were making loud squawking noises.

    birds   monkeys   koalas   squirrels

    What clues made you select this animal? _____

    _____

    _____

3.   We visited the reptile house. Many of the animals were scaly and slithering around on their bellies.

    parrots   hippopotamuses   snakes   zebras

    What clues made you select this animal? _____

    _____

    _____

Drawing Conclusions

When you **draw conclusions**, you consider the information you have and come up with answers based on that information. The answers may not have been stated directly in what you read.

Example: We saw one of the zookeepers training an animal, who swims and lives on the rocks in one of the zoo's ponds, to balance a ball on its nose. Was it a tiger, monkey, giraffe, or seal? (It would not be a tiger, monkey, or giraffe, because they do not swim or live in a zoo pond. So, the answer would be seal.)

Circle the item that fits each description. Then, write the clues that helped you choose that item.

1.   Sharon was looking for something to carry on her business trip. She wanted it to be large enough to hold her money, glasses, address book, and a small cosmetic bag. She preferred that it had a shoulder strap and would match all of the clothes she was taking.

   wallet   purse   suitcase   backpack

   What clues made you select this item? _____

   _____

2.   Sharon went to buy something she could wear after work. She knew how hot Florida could get in the summer, and she wanted to be able to cool off and relax at the beach after work. She found the perfect thing. It was light blue with little yellow fish around each leg opening.

   beach towel   tennis shorts   bathing suit   golf shirt

   What clues made you select this item? _____

   _____

3.   Sharon stopped at a store. She told the salesperson where she was going, what clothes she was taking, and how she would be on her feet a lot. She explained how she would like everything to match but the most important thing was for her to be comfortable when standing all day and demonstrating her product. Sharon sat to try on some of the things the salesperson brought her.

   hat   shoes   luggage   belt

   What clues made you select this item? _____

   _____

Name: _____ Date: _____

Drawing Conclusions

When you **draw conclusions**, you consider the information you have and come up with answers based on that information. The answers may not have been stated directly in what you read.

Circle the occupation that fits each character description. Then, tell why you chose that occupation.

1.   Veronica usually sits at a desk in the front of the office answering phones, making appointments for clients, and greeting them when they enter the law office. Her appearance is important to her job, because Veronica is the first person people see when they come into the office.

administrative assistant   lawyer   receptionist   telephone operator

Why did you select the occupation that you did? _____

_____

2.   Nathan never knows what to expect when he goes to work. Some days, he patrols his route. Other days, the dispatcher radios him to go to a specific address because of some trouble.

chauffeur   police officer   firefighter   dog catcher

Why did you select the occupation that you did? _____

_____

3.   Grant does not have an office, but he goes to work every day. He works in a tall building where he always has something to do for the good of the building. He might fix an out-of-order elevator or replace a pipe.

maintenance man   janitor   plumber   electrician

Why did you select the occupation that you did? _____

_____

4.   Tobie loves her job. On days when she does not have surgery, Tobie might see as many as 40 patients. Many of them come for yearly checkups and shots. But sometimes, they are sick. Tobie cannot always tell what is wrong from a temperature reading or from listening to a patient's chest. Tobie sometimes has to get more information about the patient's current symptoms from the person to whom the patient belongs.

dentist   veterinarian   surgeon   medical doctor

Why did you select the occupation that you did? _____

_____

Making Inferences

Making an inference means summing up given information that implies something else has happened.

Example: Keisha wiped up the milk with a sponge. (You can infer from the given information that the milk had probably been spilled.)

Each sentence implies that something has happened. Write a sentence telling what may have happened.

1. _____

   The boy's mom apologized to the shop owner.

2. _____

   The dog lay down by the fire to warm herself.

3. _____

   The animals scurried back into the woods.

4. _____

   The boys roared with laughter.

5. _____

   Tasha swung her bat even harder this time.

6. _____

   Maria counted the money left in her wallet.

7. _____

   Dad got out of the car and looked at the dent in the front fender.

8. _____

   When Armando got home, he found the bird's nest was empty.

Making Inferences

Making an inference means summing up given information that implies something else has happened.

Example: The boys roared with laughter. (You can infer from the information that something funny just happened.)

Read the story. Then, circle the phrase that completes each sentence.

Before the Atkins family began to pack for their vacation, they made a list of what they would need. Then, they laid out the needed clothes on the dining room table. They each had three pairs of shorts, three T-shirts, a swimming suit, socks, and shoes. They put their tents, sleeping bags, raincoats, flashlights, bug spray, cooking equipment, and fishing gear on the dining room floor.

1. The Atkins family's vacation was going _____.

   to be in a warm climate

   to be in a city

2. The place they were going _____.

   often had afternoon showers

   never had any bugs

3. On their vacation, they were _____.

   going to eat out in restaurants

   going camping

4. They would be away _____.

   for two weeks

   for a long weekend

They put the camping equipment and a duffel bag filled with their clothes in the car. They were off! In a couple of hours, they got to the campsite. After setting up camp, they headed for a swim. They ran shoeless to the water and jumped in. After swimming, they had to shower because they were muddy. They hung their suits on trees to dry. While Mom prepared dinner at the campsite, Dad and the children went back to the lake with their poles and bait.

5. The campsite was _____.

   at the seashore

   in the woods

6. The campsite was _____.

   not too far from home

   first-class

7. They swam _____.

   in a swimming pool

   in a lake

8. Dad and the children _____.

   brought back fish

   fell in the pond

Making Inferences

Making an inference means summing up given information that implies something else has happened.

Example: Marcus counted the money left in his wallet. (You can infer from the information that Marcus just bought something.)

Circle the situation that led to the ending described in each sentence.

1. Finally, a taxi pulled over to the curb, and the traveler climbed in with his drenched suitcase.

    A. The traveler had just arrived.

    B. The traveler had called for a taxi.

    C. The traveler had been standing in the rain trying to hail a taxi.

2. Mickey left the doctor's office with her arm in a sling.

    A. Mickey had gone to the doctor to get some new medicine.

    B. Mickey had tripped and fallen on her shoulder.

    C. Mickey had gone to see the doctor because the sling was uncomfortable.

3. The cafeteria's line was at a standstill.

    A. There were too many people in line.

    B. The food was very good.

    C. The server had gone to refill the chicken tray.

4. The students slept on the bus all of the way back to school.

    A. The class had been camping for three days.

    B. The bus had been late getting them.

    C. The class had gone to the high school band concert for two hours.

5. When we opened the door, we heard the culprit who had made the mess in the house.

    A. The wind had blown through an open window.

    B. There had been an earthquake.

    C. A bird had flown inside through an open window and had become frightened.

6. The meat was not on the counter, where Mother had left it.

    A. The family had finished dinner.

    B. Mother had put it in the refrigerator.

    C. The dog had been left alone in the kitchen.

More Making Inferences

Making an inference means summing up given information that implies something else has happened.

Use each dialogue to make an inference. Write the next part of the script.

1. Mom: Hi, Brian. How was school today?

   Brian: It was great. Wait until you hear about it. You are going to smile from ear to ear.

   Mom: I cannot wait to hear about your day. What happened?

   Brian: _____

   _____

   _____

2. Dad: Sean, are you awake?

   Sean: Wow, I am so tired! I almost fell asleep right here at the baseball game.

   Dad: Well, I am not surprised after last night.

   Sean: _____

   _____

   _____

3. Sandra: What time did Tina say that she would be here?

   Missy: She said that she would be here right after her soccer game. It should be any minute.

   Sandra: I wonder what her big surprise is. She said that it definitely involves us.

   Missy: She has been very sneaky lately, and I did hear her say something about a famous rock group.

   Tina: _____

   _____

   _____

More Making Inferences

Making an inference is like being a detective. You use the information you have to think about what may have happened previously.

Read the situations and answer the questions.

1. Mr. Jones was driving on the highway when traffic began to slow down and finally came to a standstill. It took a half hour to travel one mile (1.6 kilometers) as traffic inched along. Drivers got out of their cars to see what the problem was, but they could not see it because it was too far away. An ambulance came by on the shoulder of the road with its siren blaring.

    What do you think the problem was? _____

    Why do you think this? _____

    _____

2. Mrs. Glass worked hard to clean her house to prepare for her luncheon. She got out her best china, polished the silver, and ironed a tablecloth. After setting the table, she went outside to pick some flowers for the table. When she went to the kitchen, she saw an empty platter. There had been cookies on it. She could not understand who could have taken the cookies. Her dog would have made a mess. Her children were playing at their friends' houses. The phone rang. It was her husband, who said that he had come home to get his briefcase.

    Who ate the cookies? _____

    Why do you think this? _____

    _____

3. Sam was playing golf with his regular foursome. He teed off at the first hole. The ball was headed straight for the green. When they got to the green, the ball was not on the green. No one could find it.

    Where do you think the ball went? _____

    What makes you think this? _____

    _____

More Making inferences

Making an inference is like being a detective. You use the information you have to think about what may have happened previously.

Read the story. Then, circle the word or phrase that completes each sentence.

When Jenny came home from school, there was an unopened envelope addressed to her on the front hall table. She tore it open and read it.

Dear Jenny,

I can't wait to meet you. Your grandparents have known me since the day I was born. I am four years old now and was raised in their neighbor's barn. I'm sure that you and I are going to have many good times together. I can't wait to go on a walk with you and see your neighborhood. I'm getting a ride from your grandparents, and I'll be at your house one week from today. Maybe I can even give you a ride.

Sincerely,

Your new Pal

1. When Jenny saw the letter addressed to her, she was _____.

    thrilled   relieved   not interested

2. The letter was actually written by _____.

    her parents   her grandparents   a new playmate

3. Pal is a _____.

    sheep   horse   dog

4. Pal will arrive _____.

    next month   in three days   in one week

Pal arrived as promised. Jenny learned how to care for Pal, and Pal gave her hundreds of rides for many years. They won a lot of awards together. When Pal got too old to ride, Jenny kept him in the pasture and let him live an easy life, grazing and sleeping. Every morning and night, Jenny would sit on the pasture fence and pat Pal. He would then nuzzle her.

5. Jenny and Pal _____.

    were in a lot of horse shows   grew old together

6. You could tell Jenny loved Pal because _____.

    they were in a lot of shows   she did not ride Pal when he got too old

Predicting Outcomes

There are often clues hidden in a story or passage that help you **predict the outcome**, or guess what will happen next.

Complete each sentence by circling the best outcome.

1. Sally had worked in the garden all day. Her back ached, and she felt grubby. After dinner, she _____.

   A. went to bed   B. read a book   C. took a hot bath   D. watched television

2. Because Ms. Lee missed her plane connection in Chicago on her way to Cleveland, she would not make it to the meeting. She had to _____.

   A. call to say that she would not be there   B. sleep in Chicago

   C. go home   D. fly to Cleveland

3. The football team's star had the wind knocked out of him during the homecoming game, so he was unable to finish the game. The team tried to _____.

   A. win without him   B. forfeit the game   C. tie the game   D. finish the game

4. Sam was bored. He had been playing by himself all Saturday morning. He called his neighbor John, hoping that John could play. John was not at home. Then, the phone rang. It was his friend Jason. Sam asked Jason _____.

   A. where John was   B. when the next soccer game was

   C. what the homework assignment was   D. to come over to play

5. We let the cat out for its nightly exercise. Unfortunately, the neighbor's dog was out at the same time and scared the cat. The cat ran up a very tall tree. It would not come down, and we could not reach it. We had to _____.

   A. climb the tree   B. chop down the tree

   C. call for help   D. catch the neighbor's dog

6. The tennis match was tied when the rain began. The tarp was placed over the court to keep it dry, but after an hour of steady rain, the game was postponed. The next day, the _____.

   A. match lasted 10 minutes   B. match started from the beginning

   C. match was canceled   D. match continued from the tied score

Predicting Outcomes

There are often clues hidden in a story or passage that help you **predict the outcome**, or guess what will happen next.

Read the situations and answer the questions.

1.   Franz was walking down the path in the woods on his way to a friend's house when the path separated. Franz thought about which path to take. It was already late, and he was anxious to get to his friend's house. The path on the right was longer but was easier to follow. The path on the left was shorter. But, overgrown bushes sometimes made this path difficult to follow. Franz picked up a long stick and decided to take the path on the left.

Why do you think he decided that? _____

_____

2.   Grammy arrived for her usual summer visit. Everyone in the family was excited to see her. Eric, my seven-year-old brother, watched her unpack. He told her about getting the reading award at school and what he had been doing since summer vacation had started. When she had everything put away, she handed Eric two packages and told him to choose one. He shook the small square box wrapped in blue paper. It sort of made a noise when it moved in the box. The package wrapped in red paper with a ribbon was flat and heavier and did not make any noise when it was shaken. Eric decided on the red package.

Why do you think he decided that? _____

_____

3.   My sister never knows what to wear when she is going someplace special. Today, she was going to an afternoon ball game. It was supposed to be very hot, especially if she sat in the sun. A rain shower was also a possibility, so she thought that she would definitely take an umbrella. She was considering wearing a dress without sleeves or long pants and a shirt. She might get too much sun in the dress, and she might be too hot in the pants and shirt. She decided on the dress.

Why do you think she decided that? _____

_____

Predicting Outcomes

There are often clues hidden in a story or passage that help you **predict the outcome**, or guess what will happen next.

Complete each sentence by circling the best outcomes.

1. Fifteen students were on the school bus when it got a flat tire. The driver put on the emergency flashing lights and_____.

    waited for a tow truck   stopped to let the students off

    kept going slowly   pulled off to the side of the road

2. Not until Marnie sat down to do her math homework did she realize that she had left it in her desk at school. Marnie_____.

    called a friend to get the assignment   told her younger brother

    made up the answers   did not do the homework

3. The girls skated leisurely around the ice rink until Billy, a bully from school, pushed them into the fence that went around the rink. The girls_____.

    skated with Billy   chased Billy and pushed him into the fence

    want to get the rink manager   screamed and yelled at Billy

4. There was a water shortage in the Southwest because there had been very little precipitation the past two years. So, the people of the area _____.

    did not brush their teeth   did all they could to conserve water

    dug for well water   hoped that it would rain soon

5. The traffic light at the top of the ramp off the busy highway was not working. A police officer_____.

    closed the street   put up a detour sign

    gave a ticket to any driver who honked   directed traffic

6. Reggie hit a baseball into the street. He ran to get it and _____.

    stopped at the curb to look both ways   saw a dog running away with it

    saw it hit a car and break its window   played with another ball

Summarizing Text

A **summary** is a short version of a longer story. To write a summary, you should tell the most important parts of the story and leave out the extra information.

Read each paragraph below and circle the summary.

1. Oxygen is a life-supporting gas and a chemical element. It is found in many solid and liquid substances. Water and the earth's crust contain oxygen. Nearly half of the weight of most rocks and minerals is oxygen.

    A. Oxygen affects our lives.

    B. Oxygen is almost everywhere.

    C. Oxygen has weight.

2. Almost all living things need oxygen to survive. Oxygen combines with other chemicals in plant and animal cells to produce energy necessary for living. It makes up about one-fifth of the air we breathe.

    A. Air contains oxygen.

    B. Energy is necessary for living.

    C. Oxygen is necessary for survival.

3. Oxygen enters the bloodstreams of humans and other land animals through the lungs. Blood then carries the oxygen to the body's cells. In the cells, it combines with chemicals from the food we eat and produces energy. This process makes it possible for each cell to perform its specific function in the body.

    A. Cells have energy.

    B. Oxygen has a chemical reaction in our bodies.

    C. We need to eat food to make energy.

4. Consider the summaries you selected for the three paragraphs. Circle the summary for all of the paragraphs.

    A. Oxygen is important to all living things.

    B. Blood makes energy from oxygen.

    C. Oxygen is a life-supporting gas and a chemical element.

Summarizing Text

A **summary** is a short version of a longer story. To write a summary, you should tell the most important parts of the story and leave out the extra information. To find the most important details, ask yourself, "Who? What? When? Where?"

Read each passage and circle the summary.

1. Mom made sandwiches. Janie packed them in a basket with drinks and dessert.
   - (A) Mom cooked.
   - (B) Janie was a help.
   - (C) Lunch was ready.
   - (D) Mom and Janie prepared for a picnic.

2. The sun was blazing. The sidewalks were on fire. Everyone went swimming.
   - (A) There was a fire.
   - (B) It was very hot.
   - (C) The firefighters came.
   - (D) Swimming is fun.

3. Mara is eight years old today. Mara got the new bike she wanted. Her friends are coming for ice cream and cake.
   - (A) Mara is lucky.
   - (B) Mara likes cake and ice cream.
   - (C) Mara is having a birthday.
   - (D) Mara was seven yesterday.

4. Tom reads the want ads. He needs to earn money for a bike trip to Washington, D.C. He gets a job washing dishes at the hot dog stand.
   - (A) Tom goes to Washington, D.C.
   - (B) Tom finds work from the want ads.
   - (C) Tom does not find work.
   - (D) Washing dishes is fun.

5. Dad and Sally were making a dollhouse in the workshop. Dad held the wood while Sally pounded nails in it to hold it together. Next, she painted the outside white and the shutters green.
   - (A) Sally nailed the house together.
   - (B) Dad helped Sally make a dollhouse.
   - (C) Sally painted the house.
   - (D) The house was white and green.

Summarizing Text

A **summary** is a short version of a longer story. To write a summary, you should tell the most important parts of the story and leave out the extra information. To find the most important details, ask yourself, "Who? What? When? Where?"

Read each summary sentence. Underline the words that tell who did the action. Circle the words that tell what happened. Draw a box around the words that show when or where.

1. A young girl tries to earn enough money to save her home in Tennessee.

2. In 2002, Major Jim struggles to become the best pilot for a large airline.

3. When a small dog is lost in the woods, he desperately tries to find his owners.

4. While swimming at the pool, Leann makes many new friends.

5. Sierra learns how to dance at the end of her school year.

6. In the mountains, Cory builds a log cabin in the woods with his grandfather.

7. In Texas, a young man eagerly waits for his best friend to visit.

8. A boy teaches adults how to do skateboard tricks during winter break.

9. While visiting California, Eduardo takes pictures for his photo album.

10. In the summer, a boy learns how to swim in a lake.

11. Alan saves a trapped mouse from a hungry fox in his backyard.

12. Over two days, Mandi and Emma fix up their rooms with paint and new carpet.

13. After school, a teacher teaches her students how to sing.

14. In 2004, Valerie takes a babysitting job at her neighbor's house.

15. When she was in sixth grade, Tricia helped an engineer invent a better car.

More Summarizing Text

A **summary** is a short version of a longer story. To **summarize**, you should tell the most important parts of the story and leave out the extra information.

Write a summary sentence of each story.

1. Myra read a story about a detective. He solved many different cases. He had a partner who helped him. Once, he found a lost cat. Myra enjoys reading these stories.

   _____

   _____

2. We have a new art teacher. She taught us about drawing and painting. She also taught us about sculpting. I enjoy the class every day. I think that she is my favorite teacher.

   _____

   _____

3. I have a new computer. I learned how to type. I also learned how to draw on it. I want to use the computer for my report.

   _____

   _____

4. Sean made dinner last night. Sean cooked the noodles. He also heated the spaghetti sauce. He even fixed a healthy salad. The dinner was delicious.

   _____

   _____

5. Lena went fishing last week. She caught a big fish. It was a tuna. This was the first time she went fishing. She cannot wait to go again soon.

   _____

   _____

More Summarizing Text

A **summary** is a short version of a longer story. To **summarize**, you should tell the most important parts of the story and leave out the extra information.

Write a summary sentence of each story.

1. Hannah stopped by the grocery store. She looked for many cookie ingredients. Some of the ingredients were flour, butter, and chocolate chips. She also looked for some cookie decorations.

   _____

   _____

2. Michael and Gordon played basketball yesterday. Michael made two baskets. Gordon made only one. But, Gordon got 3 rebounds, and Michael did not get any rebounds.

   _____

   _____

3. The story is about an 11-year-old girl. Shania loves all kinds of animals. She helps a local bird expert after school. She helps rescue wild birds.

   _____

   _____

4. I have two small dogs named Holly and Pepper. Holly and Pepper chase each other every day. They wrestle too. Sometimes, Holly and Pepper make me laugh so hard that I roll in the grass with them.

   _____

   _____

5. I went on vacation to New York City. I visited many interesting places. I went to the Bronx Zoo, Times Square, and the Museum of Natural History. My favorite spots were the zoo and the museum.

   _____

   _____

More Summarizing Text

To **summarize** text, provide the most important parts of a story including who, what, when, and where. Write a new sentence using only those important parts.

Write a summary sentence of each story.

1. Over winter break, I went on a ski trip in the mountains. I had to save my allowance for two months. My mom allowed me to invite two friends, so I brought Kayla and Yvonne. During the trip, we took skiing lessons and attempted the bunny slopes. We had a fantastic time.

   _____

2. Every week, I volunteer in my neighborhood. I help serve meals at a nearby soup kitchen. The soup kitchen serves homeless people in our community. It offers them hot food and cold drinks. Working at the soup kitchen gives me a good feeling.

   _____

3. Jenna and I have played baseball during recess for two years. Last year, we formed our own baseball team. Since our town does not have a baseball league, we invited our neighbors. Every afternoon, we met at the playground and we formed teams. Then, we would play six innings. Our baseball league was incredibly fun.

   _____

4. Five years ago, our neighborhood was filled with trees. We were the only house in the community, so we did not have any neighbors. It was a great area to play hide-and-seek. Over time, the trees were cut down and new homes were built. Now, our neighborhood is very crowded.

   _____

5. Every year, several colleges enter a solar-car competition. The students design the cars, and a large factory builds them. Each design is unique. After the cars have been built, different colleges race to see which car works the best.

   _____

Compare and Contrast

To **compare** means to note the similarities of and differences between things. To **contrast** means to show the differences between things. By comparing and contrasting, you will better understand the material you are reading.

Read the passage and follow the directions below.

There are two kinds of elephants living today: the Indian elephant and the African elephant. The Indian elephant is smaller, stands about ten feet (3 meters) tall, and weighs about four tons (3,600 kilograms). It has smaller ears, a high forehead, and only one lip at the end of its smooth trunk. There are five nails on each of its front feet and four on each hind foot. Only the male has small tusks. The Indian elephant is usually the one seen in zoos. The African elephant is around eleven feet (3.4 meters) tall and weighs about six tons (5,400 kilograms). Its ears are big, and its forehead is sloped. Its front feet each have four nails, and the hind feet each have three nails. Also, its trunk is ringed, and its tusks are large.

Compare the two kinds of elephants by filling in the chart. First, write the names of the two kinds of elephants on the top lines. Then, fill in the facts about them. If the information was not given in the article, write *not given*.

Kind of Elephant	_____	_____
Height	_____	_____
Weight	_____	_____
Ear Size	_____	_____
Forehead Type	_____	_____
Number of Lips	_____	_____
Skin Type on Trunk	_____	_____
Tusk Size	_____	_____
Number of Nails: Front Feet	_____	_____
Number of Nails: Hind Feet	_____	_____

Compare and Contrast

To **compare** means to note the similarities of and differences between things.
To **contrast** means to show the differences between things. By comparing and contrasting, you will better understand the material you are reading.

Read the passage and follow the directions below.

Camels were once wild animals in Arabia and Asia, but long ago, they were domesticated. There are two kinds of camels: the one-humped Arabian camel and the two-humped Bactrian camel. Both can carry heavy loads, but the Bactrian camel is sturdier, can carry heavier loads, and can withstand cooler climates. Arabian camels, which can be trained for racing, have shorter hair than Bactrian camels.

A camel's hump is actually fat that the camel's body uses for food when plant food is not available on long desert walks. Water is not stored in a camel's hump. Water is stored in body tissues and in pouches inside its stomach.

Nomadic people in North Africa and Asia still use camels. They carry loads where there are no roads. Camels are called "ships of the desert" because of their swaying motion when they walk and carry their loads. But, camels are more than beasts of burden. Their hair, hides, bones, meat, and milk are used for food and clothing.

List the similarities of and differences between the camels using the facts below.

- store water in body tissues and pouches
- are used for food and clothing
- are trained for racing

- have one hump
- can withstand cooler climates
- have swaying motion

- store food in hump
- are sturdier
- have two humps
- have shorter hair

Arabian Camel	Both	Bactrian Camel
_____	_____	_____
_____	_____	_____
_____	_____	_____
_____	_____	_____
_____	_____	_____

Compare and Contrast

To **compare** means to note the similarities of and differences between things.
To **contrast** means to show the differences between things. By comparing and
contrasting, you will better understand the material you are reading.

Read the passage. Underline three facts that show the differences between the
players. Circle three facts that show their similarities.

Michael Jordan grew up in North Carolina. His father built a basketball court in
the backyard for all of his children to use. Michael enjoyed all sports, but basketball
was his favorite. Michael tried to make his high school's varsity team as a sophomore,
but the coach thought that he was too short. However, by his junior year, he had
grown and sharpened his basketball skills, and he made the varsity team. The rest
is history: he got a scholarship to the University of North Carolina, won the national
championship for the university, helped the United States Olympic basketball team
win a gold medal, and became a Chicago Bull. Michael Jordan broke many National
Basketball Association (NBA) records and received several Most Valuable Player
(MVP) awards. He retired from basketball and tried playing baseball, but after two
years, he returned to playing basketball and set even more records.

Kareem Abdul Jabbar was born Ferdinand Lewis Alcindor Jr. He was born and
raised in the New York City area. Early on, he had a passion for music and baseball.
Not until the summer between first and second grade did he first pick up a basketball.
In eighth grade, he helped his junior high win the district championship. Lew made the
high school varsity team his freshman year, and the rest is history: he led his high school
to record-setting winning streaks, received a scholarship to the University of California
at Los Angeles, and led the team to three titles while receiving three MVP awards.
During his college years, he changed his name to Kareem Abdul Jabbar. He also
boycotted the 1968 Olympics. He and other U.S. athletes decided a boycott would
send a message about racism in the United States. After college, he was drafted by
the Milwaukee Bucks and was traded six years later to the Los Angeles Lakers. For both
teams, he had personal and team successes. He was voted MVP five times. He was
the NBA's leading scorer and led both teams to national championships.

Cause and Effect

There are times when one event causes another event to happen. This is a **cause** (reason) and **effect** (result) relationship.

Example: April showers bring May flowers. (April showers is the cause. Bring May flowers is the effect.)

Write the letter for each effect.

1. After a week of rain, _____

2. When the car came to a sudden stop, _____

3. My bike hit a rock in the road, _____

4. With a minute left we scored a goal _____

5. In chemistry class, we mixed the two chemicals and _____

6. After the drive on the dusty dirt roads, _____

7. There was a loud crash outside, _____

8. I heard the bell ring _____

9. When the dog heard the thunder, _____

10. It would soon be dark enough _____

11. We went to the airport _____

12. The team had practiced every day _____

13. Once the lawn mower motor started, _____

14. On Saturday, my dad tripped on the doormat _____

15. The mail carrier rang our bell _____

A. and broke his ankle.

B. smoke filled the laboratory.

C. to shoot off the fireworks.

D. to win the soccer game 5 to 4.

E. to pick up our guests.

F. the car needed to be washed.

G. the river rose over its banks.

H. because she had a special delivery letter.

I. my seat belt tightened.

J. so I ran to see what happened.

K. and it flew into the air with me still on it.

L. and was prepared for the big game.

M. and ran the rest of the way to school.

N. she hid under the bed.

O. Father was able to cut the grass.

Cause and Effect

There are times when one event causes another event to happen. Recognizing the **cause** (the reason) and **effect** (the result) of a story helps you to better understand the story.

Example: Margaret fell from her tree house and broke her arm. (<u>Fell from the tree house</u> is the cause. <u>Broke her arm</u> is the effect.)

Complete each sentence by choosing the cause or effect from the word bank. Then, circle the causes and underline the effects in the sentences.

1. The overhead light of the car was left on overnight. When Father tried to start the car in the morning, the _____ .

2. Dad put _____ in the dishwasher, and when he came to unload it, there was foam all over the kitchen floor.

3. Because of the high winds yesterday, the employees of the electric company _____ to restore electricity to the city.

4. The house on the hill _____ and needed a lot of restoring before it could open as a restaurant.

5. Main Street had a lot of potholes because of all of the _____ during the winter.

6. Mom found a sock blocking the air passage when she opened the vacuum cleaner to see why it _____ .

7. Robyn kept up with her work and studied hard for every scheduled test, so it was not a surprise that _____ .

8. I heard the phone ringing, but _____ to answer it because my arms were full of packages.

snow and ice	battery was dead
too much detergent	was very old
was not picking up the dirt	worked all night
she got four As on her report card	I could not get into the house

Cause and Effect

There are times when one event causes another event to happen. Recognizing the **cause** (the reason) and **effect** (the result) of a story helps you to better understand the story.

Complete the chart by matching the causes and effects.

The regular path was blocked by a fallen tree.

Fishing in the stream was difficult.

Today, I had my best golf score ever.

It was easy for the blue team to score.

The water was running fast.

The red team's goalie was out of position.

The pitcher threw a high ball.

The hikers took a longer route.

I hit golf balls at the practice range yesterday.

The batter hit a home run into the stands.

Cause	Effect
A stray dog kept trying to eat our food.	We moved our picnic spot from under the tree to a picnic table.
1.	
2.	
3.	
4.	
5.	

Fact or Opinion?

Facts are real and true statements. **Opinions** are ideas, feelings, or beliefs.

Read each sentence. Mark it as a fact or an opinion. Then, write two sentences and ask a friend or family member to mark them as facts or opinions.

	Fact	Opinion
1. The temperature is 82°F (28°C).		
2. Gina's sister is really cute.		
3. Charlotte's Web is a better book than a movie.		
4. Jack did a better job on the test than I did.		
5. This year's carnival was more fun than last year's.		
6. It took us eight-and-a-half hours to get to Akron, Ohio.		
7. Philadelphia, Pennsylvania got a trace of snow yesterday.		
8. It is too cold to play outside.		
9. Asparagus tastes awful.		
10. Football is the toughest sport.		
11. Blue whales can be up to 100 feet (30.5 meters) long.		
12. Geometry is easy.		
13. Maple and oak trees grow in the Midwest.		
14.		
15.		

Fact or Opinion?

Facts are real and true statements. **Opinions** are ideas, feelings, or beliefs.

Write *O* if the sentence is an opinion. Write *F* if it is a fact.

_____ 1. The movie I saw last night was the funniest show on Earth.

_____ 2. M is the 13th letter of the alphabet.

_____ 3. If you ask me, most people did not vote for the right candidate.

_____ 4. The headlines of the paper reported the results of the election.

_____ 5. In the contest, I thought that Harry's bike had the greatest decorations.

_____ 6. Chocolate ice cream with chocolate sauce is the best dessert.

_____ 7. I think that the governor should make the school year shorter.

_____ 8. The elevator service in the office building is poor.

_____ 9. The fruit of an oak tree is the acorn.

_____ 10. The Grand Canyon is in Arizona.

_____ 11. The Big and Little Dippers are constellations that revolve around the North Star in the night sky.

_____ 12. The plane was due to leave at 5:10 P.M., but it was delayed due to stormy weather.

_____ 13. Canada has ten provinces and three territories.

_____ 14. The food at the diner was terrible.

_____ 15. The leafless tree looks scary in the moonlight.

_____ 16. Everyone who lives in that state is alike.

_____ 17. South is the opposite direction of north.

_____ 18. On July 4, America celebrates its independence from England.

Fact or Opinion?

Facts are real and true statements. **Opinions** are ideas, feelings, or beliefs.

Read the passages. Write *F* if the statement is a fact. Write *O* if it is an opinion.

The Great Barrier Reef is considered by many people to be the eighth natural wonder of the world. It is the largest coral structure in the world and the largest structure ever constructed by living organisms.

The Great Barrier Reef consists mostly of coral, a rock-like substance made by tiny animals. These tiny animals, called polyps, are too numerous to count. New polyps are constantly being born through a continuous cycle of reproducing, eating, and dying. New coral is added to the reef through this process.

The reef is constantly changing its shape and color. This is caused by the polyps' constant activities, and by visitors to the reef whose activities cannot help but destroy it.

_____ 1. The tiny animals that make the Great Barrier Reef are called polyps.

_____ 2. People should not be allowed to visit the reef.

_____ 3. It is a good thing that there are so many polyps.

_____ 4. The Great Barrier Reef is the largest coral structure in the world.

Tropical rain forests lie near the equator. Rain falls almost every day, and there is little variation in temperature. Tropical rain forests are packed with all kinds of dense vegetation, including trees, vines, shrubs, and brightly colored flowers. About half of the world's species of plants and animals live in tropical rain forests.

The world's tropical rain forests are in great danger. They are being cut down to provide timber and firewood and to make room for homes, roads, farms, and factories. Some areas are being cleared for the mining of oil and valuable minerals. The habitats of thousands of species of animals and plants have already vanished. The way of life for many people in the rain forest is also threatened by these changes.

_____ 5. There is too much vegetation in rain forests.

_____ 6. Tropical rain forests are wet.

_____ 7. All development should stop in tropical rain forests.

_____ 8. A tropical rain forest is a densely packed area of trees and plants.

Name: _____ Date: _____

Fiction and Nonfiction

A **fiction** story is invented by someone and may be based on some real experiences. **Nonfiction** works include all writings that are not fiction. Stories about factual, documented events are nonfiction.

Write *F* if the book is fiction. Write *NF* if it is nonfiction.

1.

The Creature from Venus

_____

2.

Martin Luther King Jr.

_____

3.

Gertrude the Jealous Gerbil

_____

4.

Marty's Marshmallow Man

_____

5.
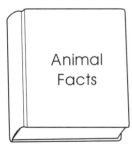
Animal Facts

_____

6.
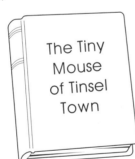
The Tiny Mouse of Tinsel Town

_____

7.
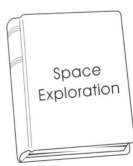
Space Exploration

_____

8.
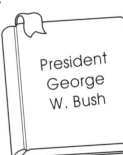
President George W. Bush

_____

9.

The Spider's Party

_____

10.

Japan

_____

11.

The History of Money

_____

12.

Benjamin Beaver's Birthday

_____

Fiction and Nonfiction

A **fiction** story is invented by someone and may be based on some real experiences. **Nonfiction** works include all writings that are not fiction. Stories about factual, documented events are nonfiction. **Opinions** are ideas, feelings, or beliefs.

Read each sentence below and decide whether it is fiction, nonfiction, or opinion. Circle your answer.

1. The unicorn carried away the boy and girl on its back.

   A. fiction   B. nonfiction   C. opinion

2. Professional athletes make too much money.

   A. fiction   B. nonfiction   C. opinion

3. Eli Whitney is best known for his invention of the cotton gin, a machine that could separate cotton seeds from the cotton.

   A. fiction   B. nonfiction   C. opinion

4. Wilbur and Orville Wright taught themselves about flight by making and flying kites and gliders.

   A. fiction   B. nonfiction   C. opinion

5. Marty and Jill were turning the jump rope and chanting rhymes as their friends ran in, jumped, and ran out.

   A. fiction   B. nonfiction   C. opinion

6. They should build a bridge across the river instead of relying on the car ferry that is always breaking down.

   A. fiction   B. nonfiction   C. opinion

7. When the storm finally stopped, Mike rode his bike to Harry's house.

   A. fiction   B. nonfiction   C. opinion

8. Weird creatures filled the underground passage and blocked Peter's path.

   A. fiction   B. nonfiction   C. opinion

9. There was not a hint of impending danger as the *Titanic* embarked on its maiden voyage.

   A. fiction   B. nonfiction   C. opinion

10. A black dog with a white ear was sitting on the doorstep when Jim opened the door this morning.

   A. fiction   B. nonfiction   C. opinion

Name: _____ Date: _____

Fiction and Nonfiction

A **fiction** story is invented by someone and may be based on some real experiences. **Nonfiction** works include all writings that are not fiction. Stories about factual, documented events are nonfiction. A **biography** is a written account of another person's life. It is a type of nonfiction.

Write *F* if the event would be found in a fiction story. Write *NF* it it would be found in a nonfiction story. Write *B* if it would be found in a biography.

_____ 1. Samuel Clemens grew up along the Mississippi River in Hannibal, Missouri.

_____ 2. The world's first atomic bomb was built at a top secret test site in Los Alamos, New Mexico.

_____ 3. When Beth was watching a television show, the electricity went out just as it got to the scary part.

_____ 4. The ball rolled over to the boys and said, "If you want to play, I know some good games."

_____ 5. George Washington Carver, who made more than 300 products from peanuts, went to Simpson College in Indianola, Iowa.

_____ 6. The earthquake that disrupted the World Series in San Francisco, California occurred in 1989.

_____ 7. Marnie took pictures of the unmanned spacecraft launch when she was in Florida.

_____ 8. The giraffe ducked its head way down to get into Theo's house.

_____ 9. In 1932, Amelia Earhart became the first woman to fly nonstop across the Atlantic Ocean.

_____ 10. When she was just a baby, Rachel moved west with her family by wagon train.

_____ 11. In 1969, *Apollo 11* astronauts Neil Armstrong and Buzz Aldrin became the first men to walk on the moon.

_____ 12. The Hershey Plant, the world's largest chocolate factory, is located in Hershey, Pennsylvania.

_____ 13. Arnie showed Ed that he knew how to pull a rabbit out of a hat.

_____ 14. Leonardo da Vinci was a painter, sculptor, architect, and engineer.

Understanding Characters

Characters are people, animals, or animated objects that are found in a story. The most important characters are called **main characters**. They seem to be brought to life by their actions. You may even witness a character's personality change as a story unfolds.

Read the story and follow the directions below.

There was an old lady who lived on the edge of town. Everyone referred to her as Granny. Because she kept to herself, she seemed a little different to some. She asked nothing of anyone and did nothing for anyone except her many dogs. The number of dogs varied daily. Some dogs came only when they were hungry and left until they returned to eat again. Some knew that it was a good home and stayed.

One day, the paper boy noticed that Granny's papers had not been picked up for three or four days. The dogs in her yard were thin and looked almost lifeless as they moved about slowly. He had not seen Granny for about a week. He wondered if she was all right.

He got off his bike and walked up the steps onto the front porch. He walked around and peered in the windows, but he did not see anything. He opened the front door slightly and called, "Hello! Anyone here?" He listened for a minute. He thought that he heard a whimpering sound, so he quickly rode to the closest neighbor's house and called 911.

When the police arrived, they found that Granny had fallen and had not been able to move to call for help. The paramedics determined that Granny needed to go to the hospital, where she stayed a few days.

While she was in the hospital, the paper boy came to feed her dogs every day. When Granny came home, neighbors brought food and flowers. Granny was sorry that she had not gotten to know her new friends sooner, but she was glad that she had now "found" them.

1. Circle what Granny's behavior indicates about her character at the beginning of the story.

    She prefers to be alone.   She does not like people.   She is mean.

2. How does Granny's behavior change? _____

    _____

3. Write three adjectives that describe the paper boy's character.

    _____   _____   _____

Understanding Characters

Characters are people, animals, or animated objects that are found in a story. The most important characters are called **main characters**. They seem to be brought to life by their actions. You may even witness a character's personality change as a story unfolds.

Read the story and follow the directions below.

Billy and Roger were next-door neighbors and were in the same class at Central School. Billy was probably the brightest student in the class. Roger was definitely the strongest and best athlete in the school. The boys often got a ride to school in the morning from one of their parents, but in the afternoon, they came home separately. Roger usually stayed and played either touch football or basketball with some of the older boys. Sometimes, Billy watched, but usually, he came home and did his homework and read a book.

One day, Billy asked if he could join in Roger's after-school games. Roger answered, "No, you are too small and not strong enough." The other boys laughed as they all headed out to the field. Billy was crushed. He went home and studied for the next day's science test.

When Billy and Roger got to the classroom the next day, their teacher said that she was going to give the test right away. That way, they could get it back at the end of the day. Everything on the test was material Billy had studied, so he had no trouble answering the questions. Billy noticed that Roger had barely written anything. When the tests were returned, Billy received a 100 at the top of his paper and Roger had a note written on his paper saying that he must take the test again. Billy offered to help Roger study for the test.

The next morning on their way to school, Roger invited Billy to play with him and his friends after school. He encouraged Billy by telling him that he would teach him how to play the games.

1. Who are the main characters in the story? _____

2. Circle two of Billy's characteristics.

    helpful   average student   athletic   selfish   studious

3. Circle two of Roger's characteristics.

    unfriendly   unkind   athletic   a bully   studious

4. Circle two of Roger's characteristics after the science test.

    frustrated   hard worker   considerate   appreciative   threatening

Name: _____ Date: _____

Understanding Characters

Characters are people, animals, or animated objects that are found in a story. The most important characters are called **main characters**. They seem to be brought to life by their actions. You may even witness a character's personality change as a story unfolds.

Read the story and follow the directions below.

Emily saw a gray, long-haired cat on her way to the park. She stopped to see if it had a collar with an identification tag. It did not. Emily walked on to meet her friends, and the cat followed her. Emily and her friends played on the swings and other playground equipment. The cat followed the girls from one place to another and watched them play. When it was time to go home, Emily waved good-bye to her friends and walked home. She noticed that the cat did not stay at the park, but rather it followed her.

When Emily got to her house, she went in the kitchen door. The cat sat outside the closed screen door watching Emily eat her lunch. Emily knew that it was not a good idea to feed a stray pet, but the poor cat had not had any food in at least several hours. So, Emily gave it a saucer of milk.

After lunch, Emily decided to clean up the cat. When she began to brush it, its fur got lighter as the dirt, along with some of its hair, came out. It seemed that the gray cat was really a white cat!

When she finished brushing the cat, Emily made some sketches of it. With a poster pen, she wrote its description, where it was found, and a phone number where the owner could find the cat. That afternoon, Emily put up her notices in the neighborhood. She also called the animal shelter to report the found cat.

There were no responses after a few days, and the cat had become her friend. Emily asked her parents if she could keep the cat, and they agreed that it was a nice pet. Emily decided to call it Frosty because it was now as white as snow.

1. Who is the main character in this story? _____

2. Circle the words that describe this character.

   frustrated   careless   caring   tough   resourceful

3. List three ways she demonstrates each of the circled character traits.

   _____

   _____

   _____

Personification

Personification occurs when something that is not human appears to act like a human or has human characteristics.

Example: The car's engine <u>groaned</u>. (The car's engine has the human quality of groaning.)

Circle the human quality of each object.

1. The clouds cried warm raindrops.

2. The wind quietly sang a lullaby.

3. The phone shouted angrily.

4. The blue balloon tickled the ceiling.

5. The flag gleefully surfed in the wind.

6. The toy soldier proudly protected the dollhouse.

7. The mailbox smiled a friendly hello.

8. The radiator shrieked with laughter.

9. The window shook from head to toe.

10. The ice cream truck whistled a happy tune.

11. The air conditioning hissed loudly.

12. The chocolate cake called my name.

Draw a picture of one of the sentences in the box.

Name: _____ Date: _____

Personification

Personification occurs when something that is not human appears to act like a human or has human characteristics.

Example: The sun <u>hugged</u> us with its warm <u>arms</u> of sunlight. (The sun has the human qualities of hugging and having arms.)

Circle the human qualities of each object.

1. The ocean waves tickled my toes.

2. The flower greeted us with a colorful smile.

3. The old pen stubbornly refused to write.

4. The gentle rain kissed my face with its soft tears.

5. The trees happily waved good-bye.

6. The cookies teased me with their delicious aroma.

7. The thunder shouted loudly to announce the storm.

8. The dog smiled and winked when I gave him a bone.

9. The lawn mower screamed in fear when Joe started it.

10. The waterfall bubbled merrily as it played with the rocks.

Complete each sentence using personification.

11. The old branch _____.

12. The key _____.

13. Jerry's desk _____.

14. The wooden floor _____.

15. His fingers _____.

16. The soda _____.

Personification

> **Personification** occurs when something that is not human appears to act like a human or has human characteristics.
>
> Example: The daisies' <u>faces smiled</u> when they received a drink of water. (The daisies have the human qualities of having faces and smiling.)

Underline what is being personified in each sentence. Then, write the word or words that identify the personification.

1. The first-place trophy proudly stood on the shelf in Charlie's room.

    _____

2. Since we could not go out to play, we watched from our window as the clouds spit icicles.

    _____

3. Autumn leaves seemed to sing as they danced across the lawn.

    _____

4. Horns honked angrily as drivers became more impatient.

    _____

5. The sun played hide-and-seek with me as it popped in and out of the clouds.

    _____

6. The clouds marched across the sky ahead of the storm.

    _____

7. The house eagerly waited for the new owners to arrive.

    _____

8. The sun hugged us with its warm arms of sunlight.

    _____

Setting

The **setting** describes the time and place of a story.

Draw a picture for each setting.

1. Time: the future
    Place: a highway where everyone
    "drives" an airplane

2. Time: the day you were born
    Place: the hospital where you
    were born

3. Time: 6:00 P.M.
    Place: a busy restaurant

4. Time: today
    Place: a roller rink

5. Time: last Friday
    Place: a circus

6. Time: yesterday morning
    Place: a football game

Setting

The **setting** describes the time and place of a story.

Determine whether the bold text shows the time or place.

1. Harry parked his car **under a large maple tree**.

   time   place

2. The policeman waved to Tasha **when she was walking to school**.

   time   place

3. **During lunch**, Steven drank a cup of coffee.

   time   place

4. Our teacher found her necklace **under her couch**.

   time   place

Complete each sentence by adding setting details from the word bank.

to the art museum	at the soccer field	in his kitchen
at a restaurant	down the busy street	in the field near my house
near our school	on our sidewalk	in the city

5. Leah went to the circus _____.

6. Cats and dogs were running wild_____.

7. The class went on a field trip_____.

8. Mario cooked dinner _____.

9. Stephie rode her bike _____.

10. Victor scored a goal_____.

Setting

The **setting** describes the time and place of a story.

Underline the setting details in each sentence. Write *T* over the time details. Write *P* over the place details.

1. Grace found her puppy in a playground last month.

2. Right now, Tara is looking through the plants at the flower shop.

3. The big city street was jammed with cars during rush hour.

4. Sampson loved last year's circus at the local fairground.

5. I babysat Mike and Ethel at their house on Timber Street yesterday.

6. Last Thursday, I learned how to play hockey at a nearby ice-skating rink.

7. In 2002, our school was built on an empty lot near a thick forest.

8. On my birthday, I shared cupcakes in my classroom.

9. We will visit my best friend in the city tomorrow.

10. I found the dog yesterday, hiding behind the swing set in my backyard.

11. Nicki enjoyed petting animals at the small farm with the red barn last week.

12. In 2006, my sister was born in a crowded hospital with many nurses.

13. Last night, the dim lamp lit the empty parking lot.

14. The clothing store was overflowing with shelves of jeans and sweaters during the sale.

Plot

The **plot** shows the main actions of the characters in a story. It often describes a problem or an important event.

Example: Gavin's father teaches him to build a barn.

Circle *Plot* if the idea is a plot. Circle *Not* if the idea is not a plot.

Example: Two sailors try to save their sinking ship.   (Plot)   Not

        The huge waves fell on the sinking ship.   Plot   (Not)

1. A small, lonely cabin sits alone in the woods.   Plot   Not

2. Two baby eagles struggle to learn how to fly.   Plot   Not

3. The hospital workers were quiet.   Plot   Not

4. Several children work hard to start their own business.   Plot   Not

5. A smart computer comes to life and tries to drive a car.   Plot   Not

6. The shiny blue car is parked next to its owner's house.   Plot   Not

7. Lyndon is trapped in a cave and must find an exit.   Plot   Not

8. Two friends fight to save a baby seal's life.   Plot   Not

9. A detective searches for the jewelry thief.   Plot   Not

10. The artist has many special brushes and paints.   Plot   Not

Complete each sentence by creating a plot.

11. Johnny tries to _____.

12. The small children _____.

13. In a few short weeks, the principal _____.

14. My sister Sarah _____.

15. Eleven-year-old Dana _____.

Plot

The **plot** shows the main actions of the characters in a story. It often describes a problem or an important event.

Example: Clarissa struggles to learn how to play the flute.

Read each sentence. Write *Plot* if the sentence shows the main problem or event. Write *Not* if it does not show the main problem or event.

1. Peter tries to find shelter before a tornado hits. _____

2. The tall stalks of wheat blow in the breeze. _____

3. Marcia adopts a pet dog and teaches it to trust people. _____

4. When Hillary is stuck in a deep hole, Stan rescues her. _____

5. The phone stops ringing. _____

6. In a crowded mall, Janice struggles to find her mom. _____

7. The icy cold soda tickled my nose. _____

8. The brick house looked frightening from the outside. _____

9. Despite his frustration, David spends two months teaching himself how to read. _____

10. Tia works hard to improve her grades so that she can sing in the chorus. _____

Complete each sentence by creating a plot.

11. While making her famous hamburger chili, Emily _____

_____.

12. In a few days, my mother _____.

13. My brother Carlos _____.

14. Our teacher, Mr. Wilson, _____.

15. During summer vacation, _____.

Name: _____   Date: _____

Plot

The **plot** shows the main actions of the characters in a story. It often describes a problem or an important event.

Example: For three weeks, Gabriella struggles with her science fair project.

Complete each sentence by creating a plot.

1. The spaceship was flying miles above Earth. The astronauts
   had to _____.

2. When I found the injured kitten, I decided to _____.

3. We had practiced our instruments every day for months. We were working hard
   so that we could _____.

4. Nora realized that her dreams could come true. So, she spent years _____
   _____.

5. Moving from one city to another was not easy. I tried hard to _____
   _____.

6. Left alone, three kids need to _____.

7. I knew that Dad loved ice cream cake. So, I spent all week _____
   _____.

8. During our fishing trip, _____.

Use the setting in each sentence to write a plot.

9. The small birdcage looked clean. It had fresh newspaper, clean water, and an
   open door!

   _____.

10. The front yard was covered with bright green grass. Around the edges, fresh
    flowers sprang to life.

    _____.

Theme

The **theme** is the main idea of a story. In some stories, the theme may be a lesson the author is trying to teach.

Write the letter for the lesson that best describes the theme of each story.

A. If you want to do well, keep practicing.

B. Everyone makes mistakes.

_____ 1. Jack was very upset when he broke his lamp. He was angry with himself. Then, he realized that his best friend broke a lamp once.

_____ 2. Sherry's dog would not do tricks. Sherry trained him every day. By the sixth day, her dog knew three tricks.

_____ 3. The first time Allison baked cookies, she burned them. The second time, she forgot to add the sugar. The third time, she made the best sugar cookies ever.

_____ 4. Gray was disappointed when he failed his spelling test. His teacher explained that it could happen to anyone.

Write four lessons that could be used as themes.

Example: Telling the truth is very important.

5. _____

6. _____

7. _____

8. _____

Theme

The **theme** is the main idea of a story. In most stories, the theme may be a lesson the author is trying to teach.

Write the letter for the lesson that best describes the theme of each story.

A. If you want to do well, keep practicing.

B. Everyone makes mistakes.

C. Telling the truth is very important.

_____ 1. Olivia yelled at her best friend, Opal, for losing her favorite book. Opal cried and went home. Then, Opal replaced the book, and Olivia apologized for yelling. The girls are still best friends.

_____ 2. Mr. Leon accidentally broke the school's copy machine. He apologized to the principal. Principal Newman thanked him for being honest.

_____ 3. Sarah did not know her multiplication tables. She failed her math test. So, she studied for five days. Now, she gets every question right.

Write a short story for each theme.

4. Telling the truth is very important. _____

_____

_____

_____

5. Love is more important than money. _____

_____

_____

_____

6. Everyone makes mistakes. _____

_____

_____

_____

Theme

The **theme** is the main idea of a story. In some stories, the theme may be a lesson the author is trying to teach.

Write the letter for the lesson that best describes the theme of each story.

A. If you are patient, your turn will come.

B. If you want to do well, keep practicing.

C. Being brave will help you achieve your goals.

_____ 1. Bethany's friends talked on the phone and traded glittery stickers. Each afternoon, they took turns deciding how to spend their time. Bethany did not always like the activity, but she played anyway. She knew that her turn would arrive soon.

_____ 2. Alex wanted to learn his multiplication tables. His friends knew how to multiply, and he wished that he could do it too. Each day, he spent one hour studying his flash cards. By the end of the month, Alex was a multiplication expert!

_____ 3. During the school play, Trey was scared to go on stage. But, he took a deep breath and stepped onto the stage. He was a star!

Write a short story for each theme.

4. Telling the truth is very important. _____

_____

_____

5. Everyone makes mistakes. _____

_____

_____

6. Even if you lose, you might learn a valuable lesson. _____

_____

_____

Name: _____   Date: _____

Mood

The **mood** is the feeling that the author wishes to convey. For example, a story may have a sad mood, a happy mood, or a scary mood. The mood can be shown through the setting, through the character, or in another way.

Circle the mood of each sentence.

1. A tear slowly ran down Bella's face.

   A. happy   B. sad   C. angry   D. quiet

2. The drivers honked angrily when the truck broke down and blocked traffic.

   A. happy   B. sad   C. angry   D. quiet

3. The sunny curtains warmed up the kitchen.

   A. happy   B. sad   C. angry   D. quiet

4. The wind was still, and nothing moved.

   A. happy   B. sad   C. angry   D. quiet

5. Mrs. Cole's tinkling laugh filled the room.

   A. happy   B. sad   C. angry   D. quiet

6. The soft snores came from the back bedroom.

   A. happy   B. sad   C. angry   D. quiet

7. The lightning struck the tree as the thunder roared threateningly.

   A. happy   B. sad   C. angry   D. quiet

8. The kids jumped excitedly when Uncle Dan came home.

   A. happy   B. sad   C. angry   D. quiet

Mood

The **mood** is the feeling that the author wishes to convey. For example, a story may have a sad mood, a happy mood, or a scary mood. The mood can be shown through the setting, through the character, or in another way.

Circle the mood of each sentence.

1. The grayish clouds overshadowed the day.

    A. happy   B. sad   C. quiet

2. As the waves slowly touched the shore, the water whispered softly.

    A. happy   B. sad   C. quiet

3. The children's laughter floated through the air as they splashed in the pool.

    A. happy   B. sad   C. quiet

4. Larry looked toward the ground and tried to hold back his tears.

    A. happy   B. sad   C. quiet

5. The clown's bright costume jiggled as he played with the perky puppy.

    A. happy   B. sad   C. quiet

6. A hushed silence fell over the crowd.

    A. happy   B. sad   C. quiet

Complete each sentence by creating either a happy, sad, or quiet mood.

7. The flowers _____.

8. During dinner, the table looked _____.

9. Elizabeth stared _____.

10. The photograph showed _____.

Mood

The **mood** is the feeling that the author wishes to convey. For example, a story may have a sad mood, a happy mood, or a scary mood. The mood can be shown through the setting, through the character, or in another way.

Write *H* if the mood is happy, *S* if it is sad, *A* if it is angry, or *SC* if it is scary.

_____ 1. Amber's hopes fell as she saw the movie star leave the set. She bit her lip as she realized that she would never meet her hero.

_____ 2. Mr. Dobson threw his pencil on the desk and stomped to the front of the room.

_____ 3. On Friday nights, Mom and I always watch funny movies. Sometimes, we even make tasty chocolate sundaes with extra whipped cream.

_____ 4. The snake slithered across the floor. His fangs gleamed in the light. Ana screamed.

_____ 5. Mrs. Greene tried to hide the huge smile on her face. I could hear the joy in her voice as she announced that I had passed the test.

_____ 6. Gene looked glumly at his watch. Through the pouring rain, he could see that the street was empty. Unfortunately, he knew that Violet was not coming back.

_____ 7. The lonely candle flickered quietly in the empty room. The walls were bare, except for one abandoned picture. Everything was still.

_____ 8. The truck's headlights glared, and its engine growled furiously.

Create the mood in parentheses by rewriting each sentence.

9. Terrence was lost in the woods. (scared)

_____

10. The builders tore down the grocery store. (sad)

_____

11. The partygoers looked like they were having fun. (happy)

_____

12. Alex lost his wallet. (sad)

_____

Name: _____ Date: _____

Author's Purpose

The **author's purpose** is the reason that a story was written.

Examples: The purpose of a news article is to offer information or teach a lesson
The purpose of an advertisement is to sell an item.

Write each item from the word bank under the author's purpose.

math book	instructions
sales flyer	sales letter
how-to-paint book	news article
advertisement	brochure

Teach/Inform   Sell

_____   _____

_____   _____

_____   _____

_____   _____

Write *T* for teach or *S* for sell to identify the author's purpose.

_____ 1. Harry's Hamster Food will make your pet happy.

_____ 2. There are 50 states in the United States of America.

_____ 3. Fruits and vegetables contain many vitamins.

_____ 4. Suzie's Super Soup is smooth, creamy, and very delicious.

_____ 5. Red, yellow, and blue are the three primary colors.

_____ 6. Last night, it snowed six inches (15.25 centimeters).

_____ 7. Our grocery store has the freshest food.

_____ 8. Victor's Pizza has the best pizzas in the world.

Author's Purpose

The **author's purpose** is the reason that the passage was written. A passage may be written to offer information or teach a lesson, to sell, or to entertain.

Examples: The purpose of a news story is to provide information.

The purpose of a brochure is to sell an item.

The purpose of a mystery novel is to entertain the reader.

Write each item from the word bank under the author's purpose.

menu with coupons	joke book
homework instructions	encyclopedia entry
movie ad	classified ad
computer instructions	sales letter

Inform/Entertain   Sell

_____   _____

_____   _____

_____   _____

_____   _____

Write *I* if the author's purpose is to inform, *S* if it is to sell, or *E* if it is to entertain.

_____ 1. Last night, the mayor approved three new laws.

_____ 2. Drake's Dry Cleaners is a very reliable service.

_____ 3. I want to tell you about my wonderful vacation.

_____ 4. Tropical rain forests contain many plants and animals.

_____ 5. The funniest thing happened in class today.

_____ 6. Our computer store offers the best selection in the state.

_____ 7. The high temperature yesterday was 78 degrees.

_____ 8. You should have heard Ms. Martin's joke this morning!

_____ 9. Tomorrow, the new principal will begin his first day of work.

_____ 10. Bart's Bank has a special package for loyal customers.

Author's Purpose

The **author's purpose** is the reason that the passage was written. A passage may be written to offer information or teach a lesson, to sell, or to entertain.

Examples: The purpose of a news story is to provide information.
The purpose of a brochure is to sell an item.
The purpose of a mystery novel is to entertain the reader.

Write *I* if the author's purpose is to inform, *S* if it is to sell, or *E* if it is to entertain.

_____ 1. Fred's Fruit Stand has the freshest fruit in town.

_____ 2. The funniest thing happened at the school dance.

_____ 3. Elephants' tusks are made of ivory.

_____ 4. Rodney Roberts can sell your house within three weeks.

_____ 5. This morning, Marie and I told jokes on the school bus.

_____ 6. When I grow up, I am going to be a famous movie star.

_____ 7. Eighty-seven percent of children enjoy watching movies.

_____ 8. Our bakery sells delicious cookies that will melt in your mouth.

Write a sentence using each author's purpose.

9. (inform) _____

_____

10. (sell) _____

_____

11. (entertain) _____

_____

12. (entertain) _____

_____

Literature Elements

You have learned about the characters, setting, and plot of a story. They are all called **literature elements**, and together they make a story.

Combine your knowledge of characters, setting, and plot to plan a story of your own.

1. Plan two characters. Write their names and three words to describe each of them.

    Character 1 _____

        1. _____

        2. _____

        3. _____

    Character 2 _____

        1. _____

        2. _____

        3. _____

2. Describe your setting. _____

    _____

    _____

3. What problem will your characters face? _____

    _____

    _____

4. How will they solve the problem? _____

    _____

    _____

5. How will your plot unfold? On a separate sheet of paper, plan the beginning, middle, and end of your story.

6. Turn your plan into a story or book. Use a pencil and paper or a computer to write your story. Then, share your story with a friend.

Name: _____ Date: _____

Literature Elements

You have learned about the characters, setting, and plot of a story. They are all called **literature elements**, and together they make a story.

Combine your knowledge of characters, setting, and plot to plan a story of your own.

1. Plan two characters. Write their names and three words to describe each of them.

    Character I _____

    _____ _____ _____

    Character 2 _____

    _____ _____ _____

2. Describe your setting. _____
    _____
    _____

3. Write your theme. _____
    _____

4. What problem will your characters face? _____
    _____
    _____

5. How will they solve the problem?_____
    _____
    _____

6. How will your plot unfold? On a separate sheet of paper, plan the beginning, middle, and end of your story.

7. Turn your plan into a story or book. Use a pencil and paper or a computer to write your story. Then, share your story with a friend.

Literature Elements

You have learned about the characters, setting, and plot of a story. They are all called **literature elements**, and together they make a story.

Combine your knowledge of characters, setting, and plot to plan a story of your own.

1. Plan two characters. Write their names and three words to describe each of them.

    Character 1 _____

    _____   _____   _____

    Character 2 _____

    _____   _____   _____

2. Describe your setting. _____

    _____

    _____

3. Write your theme. _____

    _____

4. Describe your story's mood. _____

    _____

5. What problem will your characters face? _____

    _____

    _____

6. How will they solve the problem? _____

    _____

    _____

7. How will your plot unfold? On a separate sheet of paper, plan the beginning, middle, and end of your story.

8. Turn your plan into a story or book. Use a pencil and paper or a computer to write your story. Then, share your story with a friend.

Page 6
1. untrue; 2. unable; 3. renew; 4. unsure;
5. prejudge; 6. remain; 7. unsafe;
8. unwilling; 9. recite; 10. preschool;
11. preserve; 12. refund; 13. rebuild;
14. unhappy; 15. preheat

Page 7
predetermine = pre + determine, determine
before; untie = un + tie, undo;
prepay = pre + pay, pay before;
return = re + turn, come back;
nonviolent = non + violent, not violent;
misinterpret = mis + interpret, interpret
wrongly; remove = re + move, take away;
disagree = dis + agree, not agree;
intake = in + take, take in

Page 8
1. stream, middle of the stream; 2. code,
opposite of code; 3. graduate, after
graduation; 4. proper, not proper;
5. color, one color or single color;
6. scope, very small scope; 7. zero, below
zero; 8. natural, beyond natural;
9. superhuman; 10. unicycle;
11. microearthquakes; 12. decipher;
13. subcategory; 14. immobilize;
15. midterm; 16. postmodern

Page 9
1. camping; 2. packed; 3. hunt; 4. picked;
5. Parking; 6. splashing; 7. pulled; 8. filled;
9. rest; 10. helped; 11. fishing; 12. end

Page 10
More than one part of speech may be
correct. Check that students have at least
one correct choice. 1. verb, entertainment,
noun; 2. noun, handful, noun;
3. adverb/adjective, outward,
adverb/adjective; 4. verb/noun, thoughtless,
adjective; 5. adjective, activist, noun; 6. verb,
excitable, adjective; 7. noun, relationship,
noun; 8. noun, musical, adjective/noun

Page 11
1. fiend, like a fiend; 2. leader, quality of being
a leader; 3. courage, having qualities of
courage; 4. sweet, relating to sweet;
5. front, relating to front; 6. lobby, one who
lobbies; resident, reddish, specialist, abruptly,
mechanical, patiently, carefully, happily,
generous, timely

Page 12
1. base word; 2. prefix; 3. base word;
4. suffix; 5. suffix; 6. base word; 7. suffix;
8. prefix; 9. prefix; 10. suffix; 11. prefix;
12. suffix; 13. prefix; 14. base word; 15. base
word; 16. suffix; 17. base word; 18. suffix

Page 13
Answers may vary in expression. Some
possible answers include: 1. the act of being
punished; 2. the opposite of appear; 3. soak
before; 4. wind back or again; 5. without
color; 6. cooked before; 7. not sure;
8. brown-like

Page 14
1. refreshment = re + fresh + ment;
2. undependable = un + depend + able;
3. enlargement = en + large + ment;
4. renewable = re + new + able;
5. disapproving = dis + approve + ing;
6. untruthful = un + truth + ful;
7. prearrangement = pre + arrange + ment;
8. untouchable = un + touch + able;
9. enforcer = en + force + er;
10. returnable = re + turn + able;
11. delightful = de + light + ful;
12. preoccupied = pre + occupy + ed;
13. enlisting = en + list + ing;
14. indispensable = in + dispense + able;
15. disgraceful = dis + grace + ful;
16. unlawful = un + law + ful;
17. biodegradable = bio + degrade + able;
18. recyclable = re + cycle + able

Page 15
1.–4. Answers will vary.

Page 16

1. E, N; 2. C, O; 3. B, H; 4. K, M; 5. A, L, R;
6. I, U, W; 7. D, P, T; 8. G, Q; 9. F, V; 10. J, S

Page 17

1. C. not heavy; 2. A. on a horse without a saddle; 3. B. containing little fat; 4. C. thin pieces of cane or metal attached to an air opening; 5. B. chest of drawers; 6. B. opposite of multiply; 7. B. graduated series; 8. A. proper; 9. C. lags; 10. B. lazy people

Page 18

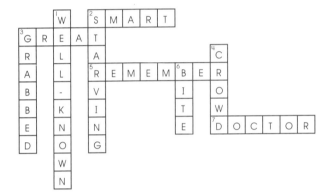

Page 19

1. trip; 2. plans; 3. required; 4. sprinkling;
5. pupils; 6. country; 7. welcomed;
8. erected; 9. finished; 10. place

Page 20

1. young; 2. forgetful; 3. moan; 4. perhaps;
5. view; 6. rip; 7. laugh; 8. gliding; 9. anxious;
10. gathers; 11. tardy; 12. party; 13. ordinary;
14. slice

Page 21

1. D; 2. E; 3. B; 4. F; 5. A; 6. C

Page 22

1. moist; 2. enclosed; 3. ignorant; 4. freeze;
5. valuable; 6. enjoys; 7. destroy; 8. often;
9. foolish; 10. reality

Page 23

1. yes; 2. yes; 3. no; 4. yes; 5. no

Page 24

1. bough; Answers will vary.; 2. bored; Answers will vary.; 3. herd; Answers will vary.; 4. through; Answers will vary.; 5. ark; Answers will vary.; 6. which; Answers will vary.; 7. way; Answers will vary.; 8. grate; Answers will vary.

Page 25

1. I'll, aisle, isle; 2. shoot, chute; 3. chord, cord; 4. patients, patience; 5. capital, capitol;
6. threw, through; 7. principle, principal;
8. heel, heal

Page 26

1. maize; 2. presence; 3. vein; 4. cruise;
5. medal; 6. beech; 7. stationary; 8. rite;
9. knead; 10. aisle; 11. lyre; 12. sealing

Page 27

1. cube; 2. pumpkin; 3. closet;
4. dozen; 5. chair; 6. star; 7. trail; 8. sweep;
O wins across the top row.

Page 28

1. addition; 2. car; 3. tropics; 4. Train;
5. Trout; 6. canyon; 7. Fingers; 8. safe;
9. blue; 10. store; 11. keys; 12. squirrel;
13. cows; 14. stand; 15. tornado

Page 29

1. lemon; 2. year; 3. aunt; 4. haul;
5. write; 6. sole; 7. up; 8. neck;
9. place; 10. stalk; 11. four; 12. vine;
13. transparent; 14. hungry; 15. pool;
16. mason; 17. court; 18. anatomy;
19. goat; 20. pride

Page 30

1. M; 2. S; 3. M; 4. M; 5. S; 6. S;
7.–12. Answers will vary.

Page 31

1. midnight; 2. mouse; 3. shiny; 4. flat; 5. swings; 6. rocket; 7. trees, soldiers, both stand straight; 8. cars, ants, cars looked small like ants; 9. clowns, sardines, both tightly packed; 10. shadows, ghosts, both were moving; 11. waves, dogs, both make lapping sounds; 12. feet, drums, both make pounding noises

Page 32

1. simile; 2. simile; 3. simile; 4. simile; 5. metaphor; 6. metaphor; 7. metaphor; 8. simile; 9. simile; 10. simile; 11. metaphor; 12. simile; 13. simile; 14. metaphor; 15. metaphor; 16. simile

Page 33

1. I know math very well.; 2. Who told the secret?; 3. He is just like his father; 4. She will sleep very well tonight.; 5. She is the smartest child in her class.; 6. She is her mother's favorite person.; 7. He is in big trouble!; 8. I would like to give my opinion.; 9. Do not get upset over what cannot be changed.; 10. You will have more friends if you are nice.

Page 34

1. C; 2. A; 3. B; 4. A; 5. C; 6. A; 7. B; 8. A; 9. B; 10. C

Page 35

1. C; 2. D; 3. H; 4. A; 5. J; 6. F; 7. E; 8. G; 9. I; 10. B

Page 36

1. 1, 3, 2, 5, 4; 2. 2, 3, 1, 5, 4; 3. 5, 4, 2, 3, 1; 4. 1, 4, 3, 5, 2; 5. 3, 4, 5, 1, 2; 6. 1, 5, 4, 2, 3

Page 37

1. 1, 5, 2, 4, 3; 2. 4, 2, 1, 5, 3; 3. 2, 5, 1, 4, 3; 4. 1, 4, 3, 2, 5; 5. 2, 1, 5, 4, 3; 6. 5, 1, 3, 2, 4;

Page 38

1. 4, 3, 1, 5, 2; 2. 5, 1, 3, 2, 4; 3. 2, 4, 1, 5, 3; 4. 3, 2, 5, 1, 4; 5. 3, 5, 1, 4, 2; 6. 4, 1, 2, 5, 3; 7. 5, 3, 1, 2, 4; 8. 1, 3, 4, 5, 2

Page 39

1. 2; 2. cuter, cutest; 3. noun; 4. 3; 5. having little or no light

Page 40

1. bald, beach, bicycle; 2. item, jamboree, irate; 3. platypus, photograph, pepper; 4. risky, romp, rumor, rouse; 5. matter, mice, mile; 6. shaft, settle; 7. thrash, tickle, threat, timber; 8. answer, anyone, apology, arcade; 9. concert, compare, condition, combat

Page 41

1. a bird; 2. wall along a waterfront; 3. a long-haired ox; 4. draw it; 5. the ocean; 6. a pumpkin; 7. sit on it; 8. eat it; 9. an animal; 10. wear it

Page 42

Answers may vary in expression. Possible answers include: 1. a large, long-haired, wild ox of central Asia; 2. It is an area in the desert where water can be found.; 3. It is a plant found in South America that provides food to the Amazon Indians.; 4. It is a warm, rainy area where trees grow very close together. A rain forest is home to many insects and birds.

Page 43

1. *Birds of the Backyard*; 2. *Night Sky*; 3. *Breeds of Dogs*; 4. *Weather Forecasting*; 5. *Big Cats*; 6. *World Cities*; 7. *Languages*; 8. *Continents*

Page 44

1. *Trees in Your Backyard*; 2. *Washington, D.C.*; 3. *South American Countries*; 4. *Traditional Landmarks*; 5. *Competitive Team Sports*; 6. *Organs of the Body*; 7. *Famous Scientists*; 8. *Native Americans*; 9. *Major World Rivers*; 10. *Famous Composers*

Page 45

1. Armstrong, moon; 2. Venezuela; 3. bald eagles, endangered; 4. scientist, radium, polonium; 5. Earhart; 6. Bermuda; 7. Napoleon; 8. dinosaurs, extinct; 9. largest whale; 10. galaxy, Earth

Page 46

1. Venetian glass; 2. United States president; 3. wolf, extinct; 4. gladiators; 5. dogs; 6. Lee; 7. Mayans; 8. Earth; 9. American Revolutionary War; 10. Confederate States, Civil War; 11. flamingos; 12. migration flyways, United States; 13. St. Augustine, Florida; 14. rattlesnakes; 15. Iron Age; 16. United Nations

Page 47

1. United States, Pearl Harbor; 2. Mount Rushmore; 3. radio, phonograph; 4. ozone; 5. clothing, late 1700s; 6. Mickey Mouse; 7. Tubman, Underground Railroad; 8. croquet; 9. cactus; 10. liver; 11. endangered; 12. immigration policy, United States; 13. Industrial Revolution, America; 14. political parties, United States; 15. chlorophyll; 16. solar eclipse, lunar eclipse

Page 48

1. 16; 2. 17; 3. 1; 4. 17; 5. 9; 6. 1; 7. 22; 8. 20

Page 49

1. 14; 2. 6; 3. 15; 4. 19; 5. 9; 6. 3; 7. 3; 8. 20; 9. 13; 10. 17

Page 50

1. 1; 2. 8; 3. 6; 4. 11; 5. 1, 11; 6. 9; 7. 5, 11; 8. 9; 9. 6; 10. 7; 11. 3; 12. 12; 13. 10; 14. 3; 15. 9

Page 51

1. Annapolis; 2. southwest; 3. south; 4. Salisbury; 5. Chesapeake Bay; 6. Salisbury; 7. west; 8. Delaware; 9. Atlantic; 10. Cumberland

Page 52

1. Mississippi River; 2. 200 miles; 3. Springfield; 4. five; 5. northeast; 6. Cairo; 7. Lake Michigan; 8. Indiana

Page 53

1. Jefferson City; 2. seven; 3. Oklahoma, Kansas, Nebraska; 4. Kansas City, St. Louis; 5. Mississippi River; 6. St. Louis; 7. southwest; 8. Springfield; 9. St. Joseph; 10. Columbia

Page 54

1. TOC: 90, Index: blank; 2. TOC: 3, Index: 18; 3. TOC: 64, Index: 68–69; 4. TOC: 25, Index: blank; 5. TOC: 39, Index: blank

Page 55

1. TOC: 45, Index: blank; 2. TOC: 13, Index: 17–18; 3. TOC: 5, Index: blank; 4. TOC: 33, Index: 35–36; 5. TOC: 27, Index: blank

Page 56

1. TOC: 18, Index: 19; 2. TOC: 12, Index: 6, 12–17; 3. TOC: 6, Index: 24; 4. TOC: 4, Index: blank; 5. TOC: 20, Index: 21–22

Page 57

1. E; 2. C; 3. A; 4. B; 5. D; 6. B

Page 58

1. E; 2. D; 3. A; 4. A; 5. E; 6. E; 7. D; 8. A; 9. E; 10. D; 11. encyclopedia; 12. atlas

Page 59

1. encyclopedia; 2. glossary; 3. atlas; 4. encyclopedia; 5. dictionary; 6. table of contents; 7. index; 8. atlas; 9. glossary; 10. encyclopedia; 11. index; 12. table of contents

Page 60

1. Birds of Prey; 2. after; 3. Wildcat Wackiness, Penguins on Parade; 4. The Reptile Review; 5. *The Monkey Movie*; 6. The Penguin Palace

Page 61

Pressing Flowers: 3, 1, 5, 2, 6, 7, 4, 9, 8; Making a Floral Picture: 2, 6, 5, 3, 1, 4

Page 62

1. 2, 1, 4, 3; 2. B, D, A, C; 3. 6, 1, 2, 4, 3, 5

Page 63

The alarm did not go off in the Coles's house, and everyone overslept. Charlie had to run to catch the school bus. When Charlie found a seat and sat down, he ate the apple that he had grabbed on his way out the door. If he had eaten breakfast at home, he would have had a three-mile walk.

Charlie was glad to be on the bus because today was a special day at school. It was Field Day. That meant that the entire school was divided into six teams: red, white, blue, green, yellow, and orange. Charlie was wearing a green shirt because he was on the green team.

Page 64

4, 1, 8, 2, 6, 3, 5, 7

Page 65

1. The Anasazi probably came to the Southwest around 100 B.C.; 2. They made excellent baskets.; 3. This first phase is named the Early Basket Maker Period.; 4. The second phase is named the Modified Basket Maker Period.; 5. During the Modified Basket Period, the Anasazi's homes were built in open areas near the land they farmed and were partly underground.; 6. The Great Pueblo Period began around 1100 A.D.; 7. The homes of the last phase are similar to today's apartment buildings.; 8. What actually happened to the Anasazi remains a mystery.

Page 66

1. B. Do not be a bragger.; 2. A. Do not let flattery go to your head.; 3. C. Think before you act.

Page 67

1. A. parts of the brain; 2. D. medulla; 3. C. cerebellum; 4. E. cerebrum; 5. A. involuntary actions; 6. F. voluntary movements; 7. G. voluntary mental operations

Page 68

1. Laws are rules that we live by every day.; 2. Traffic laws maintain safety.; 3. The courts must protect individual rights.; 4. to protect the rights of everyone

Page 69

One reason to classify animals is to determine which ones are related to each other.; Monkeys and apes belong to a group called primates.; Early primates probably ate insects, but they also ate leaves and fruits.

Page 70

1. Long ago, festivals were held when there was a good harvest; 2. The first European settlers in America had a fall festival that they named Thanksgiving.; 3. There is usually a celebration of some sort after a harvest.

Page 71

1. Ancient civilizations did not have scientific information that explained the causes of earthquakes.; 2. Some Native Americans thought a giant sea turtle held up Earth.; 3. In India, it was believed that four elephants held up Earth.; 4. The ancient Greeks thought earthquakes showed the gods' anger.

Page 72

Answers will vary. Possible answers include:
1. The Rosetta Stone was found in Egypt more than 200 years ago.; 2. The Rosetta stone tells about King Ptolemy V.; 3. There are three different kinds of writing on the stone.; 4. The Rosetta stone unlocked the mystery of the symbols that covered the temples and tombs of ancient Egypt.

Page 73

1. How Papyrus Was Made; 2. Writing in Ancient Egypt; 3. Burying the Dead in Ancient Egypt

Page 74

1. Titles will vary.; 2. When the United States Constitution was written in 1787, it established a government in which power was split between three branches: legislative, executive, and judicial.; 3. Answers will vary.; 4. Although changes have been made to the Constitution since 1787, the three branches of government remain as originally written.

Page 75

1. C. Cousins with Claws; 2. C. Lobsters are saltwater animals belonging to a group called crustaceans.; 3. B. Crayfish are freshwater versions of their crustacean cousins called lobsters.

Page 76

1. Minnie Watson had simply had enough aggravation from her old car; 2. When Crystal first climbed aboard the sleigh, she had no idea how special it was. 3. Actually, Tom was afraid of more things than anyone would believe.; 4. There are many breeds of cattle.; 5. Hugo is a hippopotamus that eats all day long.; 6. Picking blackberries was really hard work, but Jeremy knew it would be worth it when he had his piece of pie!

Page 77

1. B; 2. A; 3. A; 4. B

Page 78

Page 79

Gastropods	Bivalves	Chitons
single, coiled shells	two shells hinged together at one end or along one side	8 shell plates that look like a turtle's shell
beaches of the Atlantic and Pacific oceans in North America	coasts of the Atlantic and Pacific oceans in North America	shallow rock ponds in Pacific Ocean from Alaska to Mexico
limpets, snails, slugs, whelks	clams, mussels, oysters, scallops	Merten's chiton, northern red chiton, mossy mopalia

Page 80

1. Friendly.; 2. eleven.; 3. sweet; 4. rabbit; 5. beagle; 6. Travers; 7. Becky; 8. mean; 9. Preston; 10. Sunday; 11. Marty; 12. Shiloh; The book received the Newbery Medal.

Page 81

1. TS = Some people like the fire department across the street from our neighborhood, and some people do not.; SD = My mom and dad think it is great because they know that help could reach us within minutes. Nan's parents do not like it because of all of the noise the sirens make.; 2. TS = Every evening, Gabriel and his dad look forward to feeding the deer in their backyard.; SD (any two of the following) = Gabriel carries the dried corn from the garage to the edge of the woods. He and his dad spread the corn. Then, they hide behind the edge of the house to watch. Each evening, the same four female deer come to feed.; 3. TS = Alley worked hard to finish all of her projects at summer camp.; SD (any two of the following) = She made a tie-dyed shirt in shades of blue and purple, glued eyes onto her lion's mask, and carefully formed a monkey out of clay.;
4. TS = Tuesdays are busy for Gabriella.; SD (any two of the following) = She gets up early for swim practice which starts at 7:30. Then, her mom drops her off just as the morning bell rings. After the bus brings her home, Gabriella grabs a quick snack before she leaves for dance lessons.

Page 82

1. TS = The first Englishman to sail around the world was Sir Francis Drake.; SD (any two of the following) = Drake left on his ship, the *Pelican*, from Plymouth, England, on December 13, 1577, to travel around the world. He returned to Plymouth on September 26, 1580. The voyage made him a national hero.; 2. TS = Each class had selected four students to represent them in the geography bee.; SD (any two of the following) = Kate was excited that she had been chosen. Kate spent most of her time studying the countries of South America. She already knew the names and capitals of the provinces and territories in Canada.;

Page 82 (continued)

3. TS = The Statue of Liberty was a gift of friendship from France to the United States.; SD (any two of the following) = Lady Liberty had to be taken apart and packed into 214 crates to travel to the United States. It was put back together in 1886. The statue is recognized as a symbol of freedom to people around the world.; 4. TS = The Vikings lived in Scandinavia from about 700–1100.; SD (any two of the following) = They sailed their wooden longships with square sails and oars on their bold, ruthless raids in Europe. They also crossed the Atlantic Ocean to settle in Iceland and Greenland. It is thought that they landed in North America around the year 1000. Besides being such fierce warriors, some were farmers, traders, and artists.

Page 83

Paragraph 1: Topic sentence—Pike's Peak is the name given to one of the mountains located in the Rocky Mountains of Colorado. Details will vary.; Paragraph 2: Topic sentence—The Royal Gorge is a deep canyon that was created by the snow and rain that run off the Rocky Mountains and into rivers. Details will vary.

Page 84

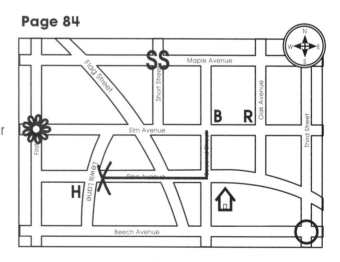

Page 85

2, 5, 1, 4, 8, 6, 9, 7, 3, 11, 10

Page 86
1. 2, 1, 3, 4.; 2. 3, 5, 1, 2, 4; 3. 2, 3, 5, 4, 1

Page 87
1. reptiles, poisonous; 2. fangs, no ears;
3. rodents, small birds; 4. Mexico, South America; 5. see, smell

Page 88
1. pioneers from New England; 2. near where Kentucky, Tennessee, and Virginia meet;
3. hunted, fished, and used dried staples that they carried with them; 4. Daniel Boone and several woodsmen; 5. late 1700s; 6. Mohawk Trail; 7. on foot and by wagon;
8. several weeks

Page 89
1. D. impeached and removed; 2. C. several hundred; 3. B. basis; 4. A. six to ten

Page 90
1. record; 2. edit; 3. Thursday; 4. Math;
5. no assignment; 6. Tuesday; 7. Friday;
8. rough draft

Page 91
1. four; 2. Cenozoic, Mesozoic, Paleozoic, Precambrian; 3. Mesozoic; 4. three;
5. Cretaceous, Jurassic, Triassic; 6. Cenozoic

Page 92
1. Asia; 2. Nile, Amazon; 3. Australia, Europe;
4. Autralia; 5. Everest, McKinley, Aconcagua

Page 93
1. Astronomy; 2. especially.; 3. telescope;
4. conditions; 5. observations;
6. constellations; 7. compass; 8. expedition

Page 94
1. atmosphere; 2. launched; 3. evaluated;
4. mission; 5. transformed; 6. distorts; 7. former;
8. theories; 9. universe; 10. payloads

Page 95
1. range; 2. incorporated; 3. natives;
4. contingent; 5. stalked; 6. accuracy; 7. weirs;
8. culture

Page 96
1. giraffe, Clues will vary.; 2. birds, Clues will vary.; 3. snakes, Clues will vary.

Page 97
1. purse, Clues will vary.; 2. bathing suit, Clues will vary.; 3. shoes, Clues will vary.

Page 98
1. receptionist, Clues will vary.; 2. police officer, Clues will vary.; 3. maintenance man, Clues will vary.; 4. veterinarian, Clues will vary.

Page 99
1.–8. Answers will vary

Page 100
1. to be in a warm climate; 2. often had afternoon showers; 3. going camping; 4. for a long weekend; 5. in the woods; 6. not too far from home; 7. in a lake; 8. brought back fish

Page 101
1. C.; 2. B.; 3. C.; 4. A.; 5. C.; 6. C.

Page 102
1.–3. Answers will vary.

Page 103
Answers will vary. Possible answers include:
1. an accident; traffic is delayed, an ambulance passed; 2. Mr. Glass; the children were out, the dog would have made a mess, Mr. Glass was at home; 3. in the hole; The ball was headed in that direction, and then it was not visible.

Page 104
1. thrilled; 2. her grandparents; 3. horse;
4. in one week; 5. were in a lot of horse shows;
6. she did not ride Pal when he got too old

Page 105
1. C. took a hot bath; 2. A. call to say she
would not be there; 3. A. win without him;
4. D. to come over to play; 5. C. call for help;
6. D. match continued from the tied score

Page 106
Answers will vary. Possible answers include:
1. He chose the path on the left because it
was shorter. He could use the stick to help
him get through the overgrown bushes.; 2. He
wanted the bigger present that might be a
book because he liked reading.; 3. She would
be cooler in the dress, and the umbrella
would shade her from the sun.

Page 107
1. pulled off to the side of the road; 2. called
a friend to get the assignment; 3. went to
get the rink manager; 4. did all they could to
conserve water; 5. directed traffic;
6. stopped at the curb to look both ways

Page 108
1. B. Oxygen is almost everywhere.; 2. C.
Oxygen is necessary for survival.; 3. B. Oxygen
has a chemical reaction in our bodies.; 4. A.
Oxygen is important to all living things.

Page 109
1. D; 2. B; 3. C; 4. B; 5. B

Page 110
1. Who: young girl, What: tries to earn
enough money to save her home, Where: in
Tennessee; 2. Who: Major Jim, What: struggles
to become the best pilot for a large airline,
When: 2002; 3. Who: small dog, What: he
desperately tries to find his owners, Where:
in the woods; 4. Who: Leann, What: makes
many new friends, When/Where: While
swimming in the pool;

Page 110 (continued)
5. Who: Sierra, What: learns how to dance,
When: at the end of the school year; 6. Who:
Cory, What: builds a log cabin, Where: In the
mountains, in the woods; 7. Who: young man,
What: eagerly waits for his best friend to visit,
Where: Texas; 8. Who: boy, What: teaches
adults how to do skateboard tricks, When:
during winter break; 9. Who: Eduardo, What:
takes pictures for his photo album, Where:
California; 10. Who: boy, What: learns how to
swim in a lake, When: in the summer; 11. Who:
Alan, What: saves a trapped mouse from a
hungry fox, Where: in his backyard; 12. Who:
Mandi and Emma, What: fix up their rooms
with paint and new carpet, When: over two
days; 13. Who: teacher, What: teaches her
students how to sing, When: after school;
14. Who: Valerie, What: takes a babysitting
job, When: 2004, Where: at her neighbor's
house; 15. Who: Tricia, What: helped an
engineer invent a better car, When: in
sixth grade

Page 111
Answers will vary.

Page 112
Answers will vary.

Page 113
Answers will vary.

Page 114
Indian: ten feet, four tons, smaller, high, one,
smooth, small (male only), front = five,
hind = four; African: eleven feet, six tons, big,
sloped, not given, ringed, large, front = four,
hind = three

Page 115
Arabian Camel: have one hump, are trained
for racing, have shorter hair; Both: store food
in hump, have swaying motion, store water
in body tissues and pouches, are used for
food and clothing; Bactrian Camel: have two
humps, are sturdier, can withstand
cooler climates

Page 116

Answers will vary. Possible answers include: Differences: where they grew up; Jabbar made high school varsity as a freshman, Jordan as a junior; Jordan went to the Olympics; Jordan loved basketball first; Similarities: Both broke records, got awards, and received scholarships

Page 117

1. G; 2. I; 3. K; 4. D; 5. B; 6. F; 7. J; 8. M; 9. N; 10. C; 11. E; 12. L; 13. O; 14. A; 15. H

Page 118

1. battery was dead; 2. too much detergent; 3. worked all night; 4. was very old; 5. snow and ice; 6. was not picking up the dirt; 7. she got four As on her report card; 8. I could not get into the house

Page 119

1. Cause: The water was running so fast. Effect: It made fishing in the stream difficult.; 2. Cause: I hit golf balls at the practice range. Effect: Today, I had my best golf score ever.; 3. Cause: The red team's goalie was out of position. Effect: It made it easy for the blue team to score.; 4. Cause: The regular path was blocked by a fallen tree. Effect: The hikers took a longer route.; 5. Cause: The pitcher threw a high ball. Effect: The batter hit a home run into the stands.

Page 120

1. Fact; 2. Opinion; 3. Opinion; 4. Fact; 5. Opinion; 6. Fact; 7. Fact; 8. Opinion; 9. Opinion; 10. Opinion; 11. Fact; 12. Opinion; 13. Fact; 14.–15. Answers will vary.

Page 121

1. O; 2. F; 3. O; 4. F; 5. O; 6. O; 7. O; 8. O; 9. F; 10. F; 11. F; 12. F; 13. F; 14. O; 15. O; 16. O; 17. F; 18. F

Page 122

1. F; 2. O; 3. O; 4. F; 5. O; 6. F; 7. O; 8. F

Page 123

1. F; 2. NF; 3. F; 4. F; 5. NF; 6. F; 7. NF; 8. NF; 9. F; 10. NF; 11. NF; 12. F

Page 124

1. A. fiction; 2. C. opinion; 3. B. nonfiction; 4. B. nonfiction; 5. A. fiction; 6. C. opinion; 7. A. fiction; 8. A. fiction; 9. B. nonfiction; 10. A. fiction

Page 125

1. B; 2. NF; 3. F; 4. F; 5. B; 6. NF; 7. F; 8. F; 9. B; 10. F; 11. NF; 12. NF; 13. F; 14. B

Page 126

1. She prefers to be alone.; Answers will vary for 2.–3. Possible answers include: 2. she became more friendly, appreciative; 3. observant, kind, thoughtful, heroic

Page 127

1. Billy and Roger; 2. helpful, studious; 3. unkind, athletic; 4. considerate, appreciative

Page 128

1. Emily; 2. caring, resourceful; 3. Answers will vary.

Page 129

1. cried; 2. quietly sang a lullaby; 3. shouted angrily; 4. tickled the ceiling; 5. gleefully surfed; 6. proudly protected the dollhouse; 7. smiled a friendly hello; 8. shrieked with laughter; 9. shook from head to toe; 10. whistled a happy tune; 11. hissed loudly; 12. called my name

Page 130

1. tickled my toes; 2. greeted us with a colorful smile; 3. refused to write; 4. kissed my face with its soft tears; 5. happily waved goodbye; 6. teased me; 7. shouted loudly; 8. smiled and winked; 9. screamed in fear; 10. bubbled merrily, played with the rocks; 11.–18. Answers will vary.

Page 131
1. <u>first-place trophy</u>, proudly stood on the shelf in Charlie's room; 2. <u>clouds</u>, spit icicles; 3. <u>Autumn leaves</u>, seemed to sing as they danced across the lawn; 4. <u>Horns</u>, honked angrily; 5. <u>sun</u>, played hide-and-seek with me; 6. <u>clouds</u>, marched across the sky; 7. <u>house</u>, eagerly waited for the new owners to arrive; 8. <u>sun</u>, hugged us with its warm arms

Page 132
Check student drawings.

Page 133
1. place; 2. time; 3. time; 4. place; 5.–10. Answers will vary.

Page 134
1. T: last month, P: in a playground; 2. T: Right now, P: at the flower shop; 3. T: during rush hour, P: The big city street; 4. T: last year's, P: at the local fairgrounds; 5. T: yesterday, P: at their house on Timber Street; 6. T: Last Thursday, P: at a nearby ice-skating rink; 7. T: In 2002, P: an empty lot near a thick forest; 8. T: On my birthday, P: in my classroom; 9. T: tomorrow, P: in the city; 10. T: yesterday, P: behind the swing set in my backyard; 11. T: last week, P: at the small farm; 12. T: In 2006, P: in a crowded hospital; 13. T: Last night, P: the empty parking lot; 14. T: during the sale, P: The clothing store

Page 135
1. Not; 2. Plot; 3. Not; 4. Plot; 5. Plot; 6. Not; 7. Plot; 8. Plot; 9. Plot; 10. Not; 11.–15. Answers will vary.

Page 136
1. Plot; 2. Not; 3. Plot; 4. Plot; 5. Not; 6. Plot; 7. Not; 8. Not; 9. Plot; 10. Plot; 11.–15. Answers will vary.

Page 137
Answers will vary.

Page 138
1. B; 2. A; 3. A; 4. B; 5.–8. Answers will vary.

Page 139
1. B; 2. C; 3. A; 4.–6. Answers will vary.

Page 140
1. A; 2. B; 3. C; 4.–6. Answers will vary.

Page 141
1. B. sad; 2. C. angry; 3. A. happy; 4. D. quiet; 5. A. happy; 6. C. quiet; 7. C. angry; 8. A. happy

Page 142
1. B. sad; 2. C. quiet; 3. A. happy; 4. B. sad; 5. A. happy; 6. D. quiet; 7.–10. Answers will vary.

Page 143
1. S; 2. A; 3. H; 4. SC; 5. H; 6. S; 7. S; 8. A; 11.–14. Answers will vary.

Page 144
Teach/Inform: math book, how-to-paint book, instructions, news article; Sell: sales flyer, advertisement, sales letter, brochure; 1. S; 2. T; 3. T; 4. S; 5. T; 6. T; 7. S; 8. S

Page 145
Inform/Entertain: homework instructions, computer instructions, joke book, encyclopedia entry; Sell: menu with coupons, movie ad, classified ad, sales letter; 1. I; 2. S; 3. E; 4. I; 5. E; 6. S; 7. I; 8. E; 9. I; 10. S

Page 146
1. S; 2. E; 3. I; 4. S; 5. E; 6. I; 7. I; 8. S; 9.–12. Answers will vary.

Pages 147–149
Answers will vary.